THE DIGITAL

THE DIGITAL ENTERPRISE

HOW DIGITISATION
IS REDEFINING BUSINESS

KAY HENNING

First published in 1998 by Century Business Books

This paperback edition published 1999 by Random House Business Books
Random House, 20 Vauxhall Bridge Road, London SW1V 2SA

Random House Australia (Pty) Limited
20 Alfred Street, Milsons Point
Sydney, New South Wales 2061, Australia

Random House New Zealand Limited
18 Poland Road, Glenfield
Auckland 10, New Zealand

Random House South Africa (Pty) Limited
Endulini, 5a Jubilee Road, Parktown 2193, South Africa

Random House UK Limited Reg. No 954009

Papers used by Random House UK Limited are natural, recyclable
products made from wood grown in sustainable forests. The
manufacturing processes conform to the environmental
regulations of the country of origin.

ISBN 0 09 927223 7

Companies, institutions and other organisations wishing to make
bulk purchases of any business books published by Random House
should contact their local bookseller or Random House direct:

Special Sales Director
Random House, 20 Vauxhall Bridge Road, London SW1V 2SA
Tel 0171 840 8470 Fax 0171 828 6681

www.randomhouse.co.uk
businessbooks@randomhouse.co.uk

Printed and bound in Great Britain by
Cox & Wyman Ltd, Reading, Berkshire

To my parents

Contents

Chapter 1

The Digital Landscape

Evolutions, they say, are only apparent in hindsight. This, however, provides little comfort to those of us at their centre. Variously labelled the information revolution, the electronic age, the digital revolution, the silicon age or post-modernism, the end of the twentieth century and the beginning of the twenty-first mark the watershed between a predominantly industrial society and a predominantly digital society. We are moving from an economy and a society based on physical products and tangible assets to one based on electronic impulses and intangible wealth. The challenge in the late 1990s – to entrepreneurs and politicians, to educationalists and economic planners – is to create a new economic fabric that is robust, flexible, prosperous, innovative and, necessarily, digital: a fabric for the twenty-first century.

THE ECONOMIC IMPERATIVE

Like all economic evolutions before it, this revolution is defined and driven by technology. As the Industrial Revolution centred around the invention of the steam engine and the pervasiveness of mechanisation, so the Digital Revolution centres around the invention of the computer and the pervasiveness of digitisation. Since 1970, two technologies critical to the invention of the computer – compression technology and microprocessor technology – have squashed more and more power into smaller and smaller areas. In consequence, digital technology has been miniaturised, lightened and embedded. Moreover, in combination with satellite technology, communications have become increasingly digital, global and

1

immediate. Superimposed on this dynamic is the current wave of industry deregulation in the western economies. Deregulation ensures that all economies are exposed to the vicissitudes of the world market and all companies to the challenges of the digital revolution.

In concert these forces are accelerating the process of globalisation and thus the creation of a sleepless and borderless economy. For business executives, politicians and economic planners, this has profound consequences. By definition, in a globalised world national borders are of diminishing influence and consequence. Rather, economic power, arguably the defining prerogative of a nation, is now gravitating to regionally-defined territories or economic 'hot spots'. These hot spots, whether California's Silicon Valley, the Malaysian Super Corridor or England's 'M4' digital corridor, are less dependent on geography to define their identity and dependent on digital communications to define their operating parameters and, indeed, their guiding *gestalt*.

As the digital economy cranks into action, this is indeed the hour for all technology companies. Many start-up firms are setting sail for unknown digital territory. Some will inevitably fail, for sustained success demands repeated failure, but the silicon industries are at the moment riding the crest of the entrepreneurial wave. However, they are also doing more than this. Their products and services are laying down the foundations of a digital economy which will stretch over the millennium change and well into the next century. Their products constitute the backbone of global communications systems and thus they provide the framework for the modern networked enterprise. To use an industrial metaphor, software has become the lubricant, if not the flywheel, of our economy. Though in hard numbers the industry is small compared, say, with energy, aviation or defence, its creations enhance the productivity and competitiveness of other industries, make possible the birth of new ones and put to death still others.

Digitisation represents a sea change in the process of communication. As such, its most immediate impact is observable in the communication industries themselves, most evidently in the media and in telecommunications. With enough sophistication, digital technology means that text and images can be transmitted instantaneously anywhere on the globe. Mundane though it may sound, communications amongst colleagues and partners and the processing of transactions themselves constitute much of the 'stuff' of what we call business. Communication and the exchange of information is at the heart of the business process whether we are designing products, negotiating deals, trading goods, promoting services or processing purchases: they constitute its very building blocks. Consequentially digitisation will affect all businesses and all sectors of the economy.

Automating each and every one of these dialogues and business transactions instantly shrinks distance and accelerates the pace of the business world. But it also does more than this. It introduces different economies and opens up new innovative space. Furthermore it creates new possibilities for alliances, opens up new markets, forces a re-assessment of organisational structure and, indeed, invites a re-appraisal of what constitutes a company's core competencies. Thus technological change will alter not only the way we do business, but also the way we think about it.

CENTRALITY TO THE ECONOMY

As an indicator of the way in which digital technology is assuming a central role in our economy, we need only look as far as the prosperity of that industry itself. The vicissitudes of business life are nowhere more apparent than in the computer industry (the hardware) and the programming industry (the software) which lie at the heart of the silicon age, but even such vicissitudes cannot mask the buoyancy enjoyed by this sector of the economy. US businesses now spend $212 billion per year on computer and communication hardware, in addition to tens of billions on software and system development. By contrast, the spending on industrial machinery is less than $130 billion.[1]

While Europe and Japan share this buoyancy, it is the USA which is driving this new economic age. It is 'the' hothouse for silicon companies and the undisputed leader in high-tech products and services. The US software industry accounts for three-quarters of the world market. Moreover, nine of the world's ten largest software companies are located in north America, where personal computing penetration of the business market has reached nearly 90 per cent, and more than a third of American families have personal computers (PCs) in their homes.[2] In 1995, the amount of money spent on

PCs, for the first time, exceeded that spent on televisions in the USA. The country's lead is augmented further by the momentum behind the Internet. Of the estimated 64 million surfers worldwide, 41 million are located in the USA. As Daniel Burton, vice president of software company Novell, pointed out in *Foreign Policy* magazine, the States 'has a robust computer hardware industry, the world's leading software industry, a telecommunications sector that is being rapidly deregulated and a strong consumer demand'.[3]

While the silicon industries continue to be a significant contributor to growth in the US economy there are occasional blemishes in the growth trend. After a 10.5 per cent revenue decline in 1996, the first since 1985, the Semiconductor Industry Association anticipated that the chip industry should grow a modest [*sic*] 7.4 per cent in 1997 to about $139 billion. Meanwhile, it was anticipated that personal computer sales would grow about 18 per cent in 1997, to 85 million units worldwide, on track with 1996's estimated 19 per cent growth according to the market research company Dataquest.[4] In many industries numbers like these would be cause for celebration, but for the personal computer and chip sectors, which two years ago enjoyed growth of 26 and 42 per cent respectively, moderate expansion is frustrating. For now, companies in these industries seem to have picked all of the low-hanging fruit. The growth rate would appear, logically perhaps, to be lowest in the States with an estimated growth rate of only 13 per cent in the 1997 US PC market according to International Data Corporation. With makers of 'plain-vanilla' PCs encountering market saturation in the USA, PC vendors are targeting the rest of the world. PC sales should rise 22 per cent in Latin America and 25 per cent in Japan and other parts of Asia.

Driving PC growth is paramount for the microprocessor companies, the Intels of this world, because the fortunes of the microchip business are closely tied to that of personal computers. In order to lessen their vulnerability to PC market swings, microchip manufacturers are beginning to focus on the emerging digital consumer-electronics products: devices like digital video-disc players, handheld computers, personal communicators and digital cameras, though it will be 1998 or indeed 1999 before these products begin to take off in a mass way. Despite the current vicissitudes of the market, analysts remain bullish about the long-term market prospects of the microchip, promising a return in 1998 to historic 15 to 25 per cent growth rates for the next decade. By 2000, they reckon, we should also expect sales of 132 million PCs a year.

Which companies then are leading out this growth? In a 1997 issue of *Business Week*, the magazine ranked its '50 best performers'. These were the 50 best performing companies in the economy as a whole, ranked from America's Standard & Poor's 500 company index. *Business Week* identified what it termed 'the new corporate elite'. Standard & Poor was selected as it has become a widely accepted measure for stock market performance, both on Wall Street and among small investors. Its 500 companies together make up two-thirds of the total market value of US stocks. As such, they are some of the most important, and most closely followed, companies in corporate America.

The representation of silicon companies within this all-comers ranking was impressive. The top 15 *Business Week* companies included seven in the computers, microprocessor and software industries, namely Intel, Microsoft, Dell Computers, Cisco Systems, Compaq Computers, Oracle and Sun Microsystems. Indeed Intel, Microsoft, Dell and Cisco were ranked the top four of the first five, evident proof of the strength and vibrancy of these high-tech companies. Quoting Andy Groves, chief executive officer (CEO) of Intel, *Business Week* noted: 'Being in the right business is sort of the equivalent of being to the manor born'[5] – and Andy Groves should know, for he himself has been born to the digital manor. Intel's growth curve makes even Microsoft turn slightly green with envy. In 1990, the company made $650 million profits on revenues of $3.9 billion, while in 1996 it made $5.2 billion on revenues of $20.8 billion. Groves has been with the company since it was founded in 1968, but since he took over as chief executive in 1987, Intel's annual return to investors has averaged 44 per cent.[6] His company assumes pole position in the *Business Week* ranking.

In arriving at its Performance Ranking, *Business Week* deployed a range of key growth measures to judge operating and financial performance. These were top-line revenue growth, earnings growth, total returns, net margins and return on equity. Thus size or market capitalisation alone was insufficient to achieve a star ranking, for being the biggest doesn't necessarily mean being the best. *Business Week* notes a case in point: General Motors Corp. Although GM continues to rank as America's largest company by sales volume, when analysed by such performance-driven measures as sales or earnings growth, margins, or return to shareholders, GM is a 'less-luminous giant'. It came in just No. 286 in overall performance on the *Business Week* rankings.

As *Business Week* noted, the top-ranking companies seem intent on growth. After years of downsizing and restructuring, many of the best managers in corporate America know they've wrung about as much as is possible out of the costs. While continuing to keep costs down, it is apparent that many companies have focused instead on growth, either through new business development or the better exploitation of existing business assets. After years of acting defensively, the corporations have turned to expansion. 'Companies are finally realising that you can't shrink to greatness,' says Eric Almquist, a vice president at New York-based Mercer Management Consulting Inc.[7]

The *Business Week* editorial noted that companies are choosing a variety of tactics to grow. Some have moved towards extreme decentralisation to generate entrepreneurialism in their ranks; others are concentrating intently on their core businesses, dominating their markets; whilst others are investing heavily in research and development. Microsoft, for example, is focusing on its core business and investing heavily in R&D. According to rough estimates supplied by Microsoft to *Fortune* magazine, the company spends about $2 billion in research and development: more than six times Netscape's annualised revenues, Netscape being 'David' to Microsoft's 'Goliath' in the so-called 'browser wars'(see case study in chapter 4).[8] More than $1 billion is allocated to R&D in platforms; including $400 million to desktop applications; $500 million to interactive media; and roughly $25 million to advanced technology and research. These R&D divisions employ a total of about 8,500 Microsoft employees.

To achieve and maintain such performance in an ultra-competitive global economy demands sound investment and access to the best talent in the business. It is a measure of America's success in the silicon field that software talent is definitely 'hot'. The industry as a whole, though, appears 'tepid,' rather than cool. For despite characters with the flourish, energy and flair of Larry Ellison (Oracle) or Andy Groves (Intel), computing is still labelled a 'geeks' industry'. Computing and software is for 'nerds', 'techies' and 'wired anoraks'. It is still, alas, haunted by the spectre of pedestrianism. This is both unfortunate and worrying; unfortunate because it obscures the creative talents and energies of software developers, or more prosaically IT (information technology) workers, and worrying because it apparently turns off so much talent, despite the riches which seem to be strewn in the developer's path.

In an article entitled 'The geek shall inherit the Earth', the author noted that the dearth of high-tech workers is forcing companies to raise salaries and dangle perks such as stock options in front of potential employees in order to lure them in their direction.[9] Anecdotes abound in Silicon Valley about companies poaching each other's talent. The shortage in the States, and also now in Europe, has sparked concern from the White House, Congress, universities and schools – rightly too, as it seems to be threatening to slow down innovation and growth in the US economy. Consequently, companies are being forced to seek employees overseas through outsourcing or by moving facilities abroad.

The UK seems to have inherited this characteristic from the States. The UK is, it would appear, in danger of becoming 'an impoverished have-not' in the technological world. The survey from the Institute of Data Processing Management, grimly entitled *The End is Nigh*, notes that like the USA, the UK is not producing enough skilled programmers and IT-related experts to supply market demand. According to the report, the population under twenty-five years old in programming jobs has fallen by two-thirds since 1990 and is continuing to fall. While this spells out a deepening skills shortage, it bodes well, ironically, for the market value of those already established in industry – and many of those already here now operate as freelance/contract staff being hired as and when required. Software Personnel, one of the largest IT recruiting groups in the UK, carried out research in 1997 into the views of freelance/contract IT staff. It showed that IT specialists who regard assignment-based work as their permanent career style are one of the biggest recruitment groups. Clive South who carried out the research was quoted as saying: 'There is an overwhelming view – 78 per cent – that the market would develop even more towards a flexible workforce. Only two per cent thought the market would decline.'[10]

Ironically, the States seems to have been a victim of its own success as a pioneer in information technology. As the 'Geeks' article notes, as technology advances it requires more and more skilled IT people to run it. It cites a study commissioned by the Global

Internet Project, an Internet industry group in Arlington Virginia, which put at 760,000 the number of software workers working at Internet-related companies, up from virtually none five years ago. This is an indicator of how dependent the US economy, and indeed that of Europe and Japan, has become on digital technology and thus on those who specialise in its development, implementation and management. In a survey of 2,000 US companies published in February 1997 by the Information Technology Association of America, the five job titles most in demand were IT-related. The association conservatively estimates that the number of unfilled positions for IT employees in large and medium-sized American companies is approximately 190,000, and that number is set to soar as 82 per cent of these companies plan to boost the number of IT workers they employ.

Thus it seems high-tech industries and high-tech skills are where the action is, but to attract more talent perhaps we need to bring more colour to the cheeks of the industry. Perhaps we need more characters like the nineteenth-century English programmer, Augusta Ada Lovelace, the first programmer in history and evidently about 150 years ahead of her time. A *Fortune* article describes her thus:

A daughter of the poet Lord Byron, Lovelace lived furiously, indulging eclectic interest from mathematics to music theory to linguistics before she died in 1852 at age 36. Aside from her historic friendship with Charles Babbage, the inventor of the programmable calculating machine, she hung out with Charles Dickens, electrochemist Michael Faraday, and Sir David Brewster, the inventor of the kaleidoscope. An obsessive personality, she became addicted to alcohol, opium, and morphine and near the end of her life got in trouble playing the horses.[11]

Oh that such eccentricity should grace the portals of today's computing industry.

TECHNOLOGICALLY DRIVEN

The economic prominence of the high-tech industries has not

happened overnight, but rather has been built up over a period of three decades. Indeed, to understand the scale of technological change that has already taken place, we need to turn the clock back more than thirty years: to 1965 in fact. It was in that year that a journalist on *Electronics* magazine asked the Head of Research at Fairchild Semiconductor Corporation to sketch out the next decade of the fledgling chip industry. Searching for some illuminating benchmark, Gordon Moore decided to plot the heady growth in the number of transistors squeezed on to a microchip, from a mere four in 1961 to more than 200, as was then being envisaged. This led to a relatively simple, but profound, observation. The transistor count was doubling every year. Moore boldly predicted that it would continue to do so for the next ten.

As fate would have it, what could have been construed as a rather prosaic observation turned out to encapsulate the digital *gestalt* of the moment. Moore's Law, as it was then dubbed, captured the essence of semiconductor technology: relentless, geometric growth in chip power. The results would eventually make electronics the world's biggest industry and Moore's next start-up, Intel Corporation, the world's richest chipmaker.

The Origins

Few inventions have changed the world as remarkably, and rapidly, as the microprocessor. Intel Corp. announced the arrival of the '4004' in a November 1971 trade magazine and described it as heralding 'a new era in integrated electronics', which is exactly what it did. Although primitive by today's standards, this first microprocessor was the launchpad for Intel's eventual domination of the PC market. The 4004, which processed four bits (binary digits) of information at a time, was followed by the 8-bit 8008. Although the 4004 had already been used operationally – for example, being embedded in the spaceship Pioneer 10 which was launched in March 1972 to gather the first close-up images of Jupiter – it was the 8008 which finally lent microchips widescale application. Significantly, in 1974, the 8008 was used in the first personal computer by a small American company called MITS.

As a single microprocessor replaced numerous other types of chips as well as mechanical and electrical parts, it meant new products could be made smaller. As the necessary size for viability shrank, and as manufacturing economies of scale rose, eventually the two driving forces coincided to produce the first 'personal' computer. From this moment onwards, the large and bulky mainframes and minicomputers of the 1970s were destined to take a back seat in the drive to full-scale digitisation. By its nature the microprocessor not only gave birth to the PC, but also to a whole raft of electronically defined products including pocket calculators, digital watches and video game consoles. More recently, in the 1990s, the twin processes of miniaturisation and empowerment have lead to the growth of so-called 'embedded technology'. As the name suggests, microscopically sized microprocessors are now routinely embedded in a whole range of domestic appliances and business technologies.

Though now positively antediluvian in technological terms, in its time Intel's 4004 chip was a model of miniaturisation and compact functionality. For example, each fingernail-size 4004 chip had roughly the same computing power as ENAIC, the world's first real computer which was almost as big as a two-car garage when it was built in 1946. It cost $500,000 and had 17,468 vacuum tubes or valves, was eight feet high by 80 feet long and weighed 30 tons. In 1946 it cost $500,000. Twenty years later, in the late 1960s, similar calculators based on transistors were about the size and weight of a PC, required a mains power supply, had more than a thousand components and cost about $500. A further decade later, microchip-based calculators were the size of credit cards, had only four components, were powered by light and cost about $5.

The perspicacity of Gordon Moore's early observation is now apparent. The first microprocessor chip, the 4004, initially cost $200, was composed of 2,300 transistors and operated at 0.06 MIPS (millions of instructions per second). Fourteen year later in October 1985, the then state-of-the-art i386 processor cost $299, with 275,000 transistors and a capacity of 5 MIPS. By March 1995, the Pentium Pro had been launched costing $974, with a mind-boggling 5.5 million transistors and 300 MIPS.[12]

To fit more chips on the same sliver of silicon, each one has to be made smaller, which means etching finer and finer lines on it. This art is being further and further refined. In 1996, for example, Intel's Fab 10 microprocessor factory in Leixlip, outside Dublin in Ireland, manufactured Pentium chips with 0.6 micron lines, where a micron is a millionth of a metre. Today, the world's microprocessor population has swollen to over 15 billion. That's more than two silicon chips for every person on Earth.

Thus ever since Intel's first microprocessor appeared in 1971, these slivers of silicon, with a host of transistors embedded in them, have grown more powerful by giant leaps, and this growth shows no immediate signs of abating. It is projected that the 886, to debut in the year 2000, will have 15 million transistors and operate at 1,000 MIPS. If this projection is realised, the computing power, and thus speed of processing and communication, will have increased from 0.06 MIPS in 1971 to 1,000 MIPS in 2000, that is, 16,500 times in about thirty years. Andy Groves, CEO of Intel, predicts that this inexorable march will continue for at least fifteen years, perhaps thirty – by 2011, he envisages microprocessors with a billion transistors that will achieve speeds of 100,000 MIPS.

This rapid shrinking in feature size, stunning though it is, cannot go on forever; the atomic structure of matter itself imposes fairly fixed limits on how miniscule transistors can become. However, it is unlikely that physical limits will signal the end of silicon innovation. The corollary to Moore's Law was that the cost of a given amount of computer power drops 50 per cent every 18 months or so. The implication being that new applications which had previously been uneconomical now become economically viable. Quoted in 1996, Moore observed: 'The market is phenomenally elastic. . . In a decade it will be possible to cram the power of today's supercomputers on to a chip costing a few hundred bucks.'[13]

To boggle the mind further, not only will microprocessors become smaller and smaller, but there will be more and more of them – lots more, everywhere. Invaders from Mars could be forgiven for thinking we are addicted to speed. The combination of geometric growth in the number of transistors packed on to a chip and the growth in the number of chips in electronic goods and applications means that global computing power and speed is unremittingly on the up. Indeed, it has been estimated that between December 1996 and December 1999 chipmakers will churn out as much computing power as the sum of what now exists. Small wonder that observers draw a parallel between electricity in the industrial age and the role of microprocessors in the information age.

This mushrooming growth has been exceptionally good news for Intel. It is now the world's biggest and richest chip company, with a valuation approaching $100 billion: close to the combined worth of the world's three largest car manufacturers.[14] Intel's fabrication plant number 14, currently being constructed in Leixlip, will produce Pentium and Pentium Pro microprocessors by the million to power more than 80 per cent of the world's computers. This is now an industry worth $40 billion a year, but entering it is not for the faint-hearted. Already, according to Gordon Moore, chipmaking is the world's most expensive real estate speculation. Turning silicon wafers into microprocessors costs $1 billion per acre of silicon, and whereas the 4004 could be made in a factory costing only $1 million, today's equivalent costs $1 billion. Evidently the stakes are high at the high-tech table.

The Feel of Change

The difference in tempo and in tone between the industrial economy and the digital economy can perhaps be illustrated most graphically by literary insights.

Described on its dust-jacket as 'an exceptionally frank and vigorous novel about working-class life in Nottingham', Alan Sillitoe's novel, *Saturday Night and Sunday Morning*, was first published in the autumn of 1958. One of the key features of the book is its description of factory life in 1950s Britain, long before the words 'software' and 'programmer' were even invented. It catches the feel of the end of the industrial era, the atmosphere and the materiality of factory life, so recognisably descended from the mechanical imperatives of the nineteenth century.

With reference to the novel's central character, Arthur Seaton, Alan Sillitoe describes the atmosphere in the factory on a typical Monday morning:

He smiled to himself, and picked up a glittering steel cylinder from the top box of a pile beside him, and fixed it into the spindle. He jettisoned his cigarette into the sud-pan, drew back the capstan, and swung the turret on to its broadest drill. Two minutes passed while he contemplated the precise position of tools and cylinder; finally he spat on to both hands and rubbed them together, then switched on the sud-tap from the movable brass pipe, pressed a button that set the spindle running, and ran in the drill to a neat chamfer. Monday morning had lost its terror.[15]

Writing thirty years later, the novelist David Lodge, describes a not too dissimilar environment in his book, *Nice Work*, set in the fictional, middle England town of Rummidge. Early in the book, Vic Wilcox, the managing director of a struggling engineering firm, is showing a university lecturer, Robyn Penrose, round his foundry. At this time, January 1986, the words 'software' and 'programmer' have both permeated the English language, though not yet the word 'Internet'. This is still some five years away.

In Vic Wilcox's none-too-progressive factory, a computer-controlled machine has been installed. David Lodge describes Dr Penrose's reaction to it:

Robyn peered through a Perspex window and watched things moving round and going in and out in sudden spasms, lubricated by spurts of a liquid that looked like milky coffee. 'What's it doing?' 'Machining cylinder heads. Beautiful, isn't it?' 'Not the word I'd choose.' There was something uncanny, almost obscene, to Robyn's eyes, about the sudden, violent, yet controlled movements of the machine, darting forward and retreating, like some steely reptile devouring its prey or copulating with a passive mate.[16]

The two characters go on to exchange views about the merits of computerised machines. Vic observes that one day there will be lightless factories full of computer-controlled machines operating twenty-four hours a day. He notes that they already have them in the States and in Scandinavia. Robyn thinks such machine-controlled factories 'a creepy idea' and ventures to ask if the managing director will also, one day, be a computer tool sitting in a dark office. With an interest in self-preservation, Vic thinks not. 'O brave new world,' says Robyn, 'where only the managing directors have jobs.'

Ten years on again and factory life of the 1990s bears no relationship whatsoever to that in the world of Arthur Seaton or indeed Vic Wilcox. The difference is most stark, and the transition from the industrial economy to the digital economy most dramatic, when the 'surreal' atmosphere of a microchip factory is contrasted to that of our 1950s factory. A *Guardian* newspaper report describes the so-called Fab 14, the microprocessor factory being constructed in Leixlip, just outside Dublin, in 1996 by the microchip manufacturer, Intel:

... by the end of 1998, the building's windswept interior will be more than a thousand times cleaner than a hospital operating theatre. In it, technicians covered from head to foot in space-age Gore-Tex uniforms will etch lines more than 300 times thinner than the width of a human hair on silicon wafers that are 99.99999 per cent pure. Here, an unprotected sneeze could cost $150,000 in lost production . . . Vibration has to be eliminated, which means driving hundreds of concrete pillars into the bedrock. The air has to be made and kept clean so that there are no particles of smoke or dust floating around – which means changing the air in the clean room six times per minute.[17]

No cigarettes and no spitting here!

BEDDING THE NET

The pervasiveness of the microprocessor and widespread automation of the workplace would have been revolutionary enough, but another development occurred between the 1980s and the 1990s which was to change the whole nature of the factory game and indeed the very dynamics of business life. That was the Internet – not just an individual computer, not just a local or regional network of computers, but an inter-connected worldwide computer network. This was connectivity on a colossal scale as we had never seen it before. Only by charting its rise can we begin to see the fundamental nature of the changes it has set in train.

The Media Squeeze

Our distraction from the television screen can be traced to the 1980s: to microelectronic developments, advances in satellite technology, enhanced signal compression capabilities and to the increased sophistication of communications technology. From the innovative application of those developments rose a worldwide industry in console-based video games; the PC industry; and the introduction of satellite and cable television and the multimedia CD.

Compression technology and industry standardisation came together in the early 1990s to create what was termed a compelling new 'platform' or a 'new media' – the multimedia CD. Seamlessly combining different media forms – newspapers, magazines, books, reports, television and films – into one multimedia milieu, it stirred the inspiration of many 'new media' pioneers who went on to develop products for both the consumer and business markets. Previously the preserve of the music and information industries, the CD found for itself a new lease of life and a new destiny.

Symbolically, this destiny was centred round the PC and not the home stereo system – though this may come full circle in the late 1990s with the new generation of 'super' CDs – digital versatile discs (DVDs) – which are both a TV-based and a computer-based technology. Instead of just sound or text on a CD as in the 1980s, compression technology in the 1990s meant that sound, text and moving images, with varying degrees of refinement and sophistication, could be played from a CD using 'multimedia enhanced' computer technology.

After a number of format wars and compatibility scuffles, the industry settled on what was termed the CD-ROM as effectively the standard format. As the name suggests, this format played only on a PC complete with CD-ROM drive; in other words it was a product with a clear computer pedigree, with software developers traditionally associated with the computing industry among its first enthusiasts. Like the Internet, the early pioneering days of the multimedia CD were the province of the computing industry although, with time, the 'content' industry followed suit and brought with it its talented antecedents.

Like playing video games, accessing multimedia CDs is a 'close-up and personal' experience. It is highly interactive, one-to-one, and therefore achieves a high degree of intimacy and participant intensity. Like the Internet, it yearns for engagement. It needs to be driven. By contrast, in 'passive' entertainment, traditionally associated with television, the viewer wishes to be chauffeured around. Part of the reason why the Internet has caught people's imagination is the ease with which one can cruise cyberspace. The ability to move effortlessly from cyber-locale to cyber-locale, to indulge our curiosity by mouse-clicking our way through cyberspace, has surely contributed to the appeal of the medium.

Compared with the traditional music, publishing, entertainment and broadcasting industries, the multimedia CD business – like the Internet – is still an embryonic industry, although it has made great strides in the last five years in terms of technical standardisation, platform compatibility, the maturing of development and distribution strategies, and in creating products which match a market need. It preceded the rise of the Internet and, together with early R&D into interactive television, laid the groundwork for interactive design and the foundation for multimedia product development.

While multimedia CD developments were happening at the forefront of the new media industry, something was happening in the backrooms of the computer industry and within the academic community. Instead of being poured on to a silver disc and distributed by conventional entertainment distribution channels, that same sound, text and moving image was being accessed via a cable or phone line, thus providing a link to a worldwide network of 'host computers' and to the content and communication facilities we now call the Internet.

By 1995, the energy and enthusiasm generated for the multimedia CD had, to a degree, been engulfed by the hype and drive which accompanied the rise of the Internet. The Internet, or more colloquially the Net, stole the limelight from the multimedia CD business. While both combine various media forms and demand high degrees of interactivity – they need to be 'driven' – the Internet seems more instant, more global, more dynamic, more connected and, in many ways, more glamorous. Consequentially it has attracted considerable talent from the design industries, from software developers, publishers, sound engineers, advertisers, business executives, marketing directors, lawyers, copyright experts and media people.

By 1996 the roots of the Internet in the defence industry of the 1960s, and in the academic community of the 1970s and 1980s, had been more or less obscured by subsequent developments. The forces of commercialisation were then more evident and an erstwhile 'suck it and see' approach had given way to serious business plans and hard commercial thinking. Come 1997 it was certainly no longer a fad, if it had ever been one. It was, in its own right, a phenomenon. With the creation of the Web as a large segment of the Internet, with the rise of online and Internet service providers and with the standardisation of protocols, the Internet is now one of the fastest growing communication media in the world. It is, though, much more than this. It has been variously described as a conference forum, a shopping arcade, a concert hall, a commercial mall, a broadcast channel, a networking meeting, a lecture theatre and a gaming zone. It is all of these – in different ways and at different stages of development.

As all of us know who regularly surf and dive, the key limitation to the Internet as a medium is the restricted bandwidth – and thus the slothful delivery of images and text to the screen. Even with Intel's latest MMX technology, an ISDN line (integrated services digital network line) and access to low-traffic periods on the network, interacting with the Net can be painfully slow. However, despite these limitations, much ingenuity and innovation has surrounded the development of information, entertainment and commercial sites which successfully combine elements of multi-media, and the explosion of growth will undoubtedly continue.

The explosion of growth on the Internet is evident from some of the figures, approximate though they necessarily are. There was an estimated one million people actively online worldwide in December 1994 compared with over 40 million in May 1997.[18] In its 1996 report, the company Durlacher projected that by 2002 more than 200 million people worldwide would be connected to the Internet,[19] and a report released by the market research and consultancy firm, Datamonitor, forecast that the European market for online services will grow nine-fold over the next five years. The report estimated that online subscription revenues would rise from $1.3 billion in 1997 to almost $9.1 billion in 2001.[20]

Maturity, they say, is a question of perspective, and whichever angle you view it from, new media seems to have outgrown its childhood years and taken adolescence by storm. Laying down an indicator of maturity, John Doerr, of Kliner, Perkins, Caufield & Byers, was quoted as saying 'technology is in its post-garage phase'.[21] He was paraphrasing his belief that new media entrepreneurs have now outgrown their childhood years of experimentation and are looking to adulthood and the prospect of solid business enterprise.

Commercially Engulfed

The underlying ethos of the Internet was to create a free, and freely accessible, global community-based communications forum. While this egalitarian spirit still inhabits the Internet, it has been engulfed in the last two years by commercial interests and a less anarchic structure. The Net has two main commercial impacts, the first being in the development of electronic retail commerce where a virtual presence on the Net will complement, or supersede, a physical presence in the high street. Such an Internet presence means that the customer base of any business is instantaneously global, rather than necessarily local. Moreover, where the 'goods' to be supplied are themselves digitally generated, for example, news digests, financial information, computer software, television programmes, feature films, computer games and so on (that is, media as broadly understood), then they can also be delivered anywhere on the globe virtually instantaneously.

Second, it is predicted that business-to-business trading on the Net will be far more prolific and lucrative than retail commerce. Not only can a company's supplier and distributor transactions migrate, at least in part, to the Net, but also much of its own research, development and prototyping functions can permanently inhabit the virtual world.

In terms of the retail market, Datamonitor have forecast that the European Internet shopping market is expected to rise from $75 million to $3.3 billion in 2001,[22] while Forrester Research, a research and consultancy firm based in Cambridge, Massachusetts, expects online American retail sales of the key products – computer products, travel, entertainment, clothing, gifts, and food and drink – to rise from $518 million in 1996 to $6.6 billion in the next four years.[23] Meanwhile, Web advertising revenues totalled $129.5 million in the first quarter of 1997, a rise of over three-fold for the same period in 1996.[24]

While impressive growth is anticipated in almost all quarters, including for example in e-entertainment, e-commerce, e-banking and e-information, the exact nature of the business model, or models, which will prevail is uncertain. As with the multimedia CD business, after the initial flush of enthusiasm, the difficulties of actually generating revenues from this medium are now becoming apparent. For example, analysts at Goldman Sachs estimate that electronic retailing is an industry currently worth somewhat more than $5 billion in the USA. This represents a more bullish analysis than Forrester Research, but is still a minuscule fraction of total retail sales. However Killen & Associates, a US-based firm of analysts, predict that monetary value of retail transactions via the Internet will expand to more than $35 billion by the year 2005.

This optimistic prediction is based on the recognition that all the elements that make electronic commerce a reality are now in place – low-cost 'merchant server' applications, credit card security systems and innovative fulfilment systems.

While there is action enough there for many Hollywood movies, most of the major research and consultancy firms are placing their financial bets on business-to-business trading, rather than retail commerce, as the Internet's true commercial springboard. According to Forrester Research, business-to-business electronic commerce will represent $66 billion in US-related Internet revenue by the year 2000, compared with $10 million in 1996. Forrester further predicts that the overall US Internet economy, including infrastructure, access, business-to-business trading, consumer retail, financial services and content, will reach $200 billion in 2000, compared with $15 billion in 1996. According to Forrester analyst Julie Horkan Meringer, 'Driving the growth in online trade will be companies shifting from traditional electronic data interchange (EDI) to more open, standards-based and easier-to-implement Internet commerce solutions. This, coupled with the dramatic cost advantage of hooking up to the Internet versus the high cost of end-to-end proprietary EDI solutions will spawn widespread adoption.'[25]

The surging growth of the Internet has a further commercial consequence: the growth in the software and hardware businesses associated with it. The Net is providing much of the current economic buoyancy associated with the high-tech sector, and is most notably a fertile spawning ground for new software ideas. The energy of start-up companies is most apparent in this sector. It used to be that the software market was an orderly affair in which a few players called the shots, but as the Internet has grown into a $1 billion plus software business, competitive white space has opened up and huge new tracts of virtual territory are up for grabs.

Software to operate online stores, track advertising, 'broadcast' information, 'interrogate' powerful relational databases, and manipulate audio and video clips or digital 'objects' was developed in 1996 and 1997. Software 'agents' which are programmed to locate, select and deliver a pre-specified piece of information from the ocean of digital data which is the Internet, will increase in significance. These 'digital assistants' ferret out the information requested, in the time frame specified and deliver accordingly.

The late 1990s will also see the prevalence of a new breed of Web software called 'merchant servers'. As the term suggests, this software will provide a range of services for electronic trading from electronic product display and search, to customer credit identification, order processing, secure payment transactions, customised micromarketing and report generation.

Neural computing and artificial intelligence techniques lie behind many of the sophisticated search engines and intelligent agents found on the Internet and corporate intranets. For example, products from Autonomy, a UK Cambridge-based intelligent agent pioneer, include server products designed to deliver personalised information to Internet and intranet users in a dynamic fashion. They use the dynamic reasoning engine technology developed by Cambridge Neurodynamics, a recognised world leader in the application of neural networks and pattern recognition technologies.

A dramatic rise in the volume of electronic trade and commerce demands that traders and customers perceive commercial transactions to be secure and confidential. Moreover it also demands a far wider access to the Net – both in business and for individual consumers, but particularly for the latter – for surfing the Net, like surfing the ocean waves, is still a predominantly minority activity. One of the primary reasons for this is that it is only accessible via a PC and while an estimated one million households in the UK have an 'Internet-ready' PC, that leaves approximately 20 million excluded from the market. As Jim Clark, chairman of Netscape said on launching his new company, Navio Communications, in August 1996, 'There's a market of over 500 million consumers on the non-PC arena in the next five years.'[26] It is a fact that far more people are excluded than included. Hardly a paradigm for mass-market activity.

This position will undoubtedly change. Indeed, many companies with large investments at stake intend to do exactly this. They want to migrate Internet access from its erstwhile exclusive PC preserve to an array of everyday appliances – the television, the mobile phone, wristwatches, the car, the CD player. It was this ambition – to embed Internet access in common artefacts – that provided the *raison d'être* for the creation of Navio. The logic behind Microsoft's purchase of WebTV Networks, a Silicon Valley company which has developed technology to enable consumers to surf the Net from their television sets, now also becomes more apparent.

Net Extensions

Up to three or four years ago, companies tended to talk about IT solely as a way to cut costs through the automation of manual tasks such as order processing and database management. However, the role of computing is now changing rapidly. It is still designed to support efficiency through the automation of manual tasks – a tactical role – but it is also now driving the nature of business – a strategic role. Mere automation will pale into insignificance as companies begin to see that information technology enables them to operate on the fly, with business units set up and disbanded dynamically to meet a new opportunity.

As electronic communications and networked arrangements become central to the process of business, so the IT function becomes more strategic. The next wave of developments – electronic commerce, online home shopping and network computing – will make this more apparent. Business executives realise that the way to increase profits is no longer solely, or primarily, through automation and efficiency, but through efficacy: speed of response, the application of knowledge, respect and appreciation of the customer and a slick, integrated operation.

Not only is the Internet a phenomenon in its own right, but its architectural characteristics and its open standards have also paved the way for the development of erstwhile local or wide area computing networks into seamlessly global networks. While limited by bandwidth and, ironically, rising demand (and thus access bottlenecks), the Internet represents more than just a commercial arena. It also represents a global computing network upon which both intranets (corporate networks that run on the same kind of software as the Internet) and extranets (semi-private company networks also based on Internet architecture) can piggy-back with relatively little additional investment. The Net changes the rules for information technology and, as we have seen, the power position of IT workers. Electronic commerce, intranets and the convergence of computer and telecommunications offer new ways to use IT. A possible shift to low-cost desktop devices – network computers and NetPCs – and the rise of mobile computing are also part of this larger mutation.

While EDI architecture was well established in business prior to the rise of the Internet, its great disadvantage was its proprietary nature and its inability economically and seamlessly to weave together an array of incompatible legacy systems. Referring to the manufacturing industry, David Upton and Andrew McAfee noted in 1996 that 'Even highly sophisticated companies have found – and continue to find – the task of creating seamless electronic networks of lean, computer-integrated manufacturing operations to be frustrating and difficult.'[27] They go on to observe that the three main technologies that companies have employed to create the 'virtual factory' – EDI, proprietary groupware (such as Lotus Notes) and dedicated wide-area networks – are insufficient on their own to make this type of network manufacturing community possible. 'Proprietary and disparate standards make such a network extraordinarily expensive, complex, inelegant and, in the long run, dysfunctional.' However, they maintain that adopting open standards based on protocols established for the Internet, and astutely implementing an integrated system configuration, open up opportunities for truly networked business operations.

The Net provides the possibility of conjoining a set of previously incompatible, proprietary and so-called 'legacy' systems into one seamless communication and transaction network. Moreover, true to its roots, the Internet – and thus intranets and extranets – are accessible to all businesses regardless of size. For those of us who believe in both the 'small guy' and meritocracy – and indeed in competition – this represents a paradigm shift in the dynamics of trade and commerce which we should welcome with open arms. Nothing in this world is perfect, and size and money are not without consequence in the commercial world, but the Net, in its widest sense, certainly opens up the playing field.

The amounts of corporate money currently being invested in hardware and software are an indication of the momentum behind this to build fully networked enterprises. According to International Data Corp. the total global software market was expected to grow to just over $120 billion in 1997.[28] At the moment the amount of money spent by companies on software to develop Internet applications is minuscule compared with their total software spend, but all the forecasts point to rapid growth. The American group, Yankee Inc., estimates that companies spent half a billion dollars on software tools to develop Internet applications in 1996 and an additional $400 million on software for intranets. In 1997 extranets will join the mix as companies pull customers and suppliers on to their private networks. All combined, Internet software sales will shortly triple, to \$3 billion, predicts Yankee Group analyst Brian Murphy.[29]

White Water Rafting

Few doubt that a sea change is upon us. A common characteristic of great sea changes is dramatic upheaval while the tide regroups and sorts itself out. Once the flood begins, no matter which way it flows, the myriad players will try to ride the wave as best they can — and hope they are positioned to catch the crest. This dramatic upheaval is currently most apparent in the industries where economic value is central to the communication process — primarily telecommunication companies, computer companies and satellite technology companies. Their prosperity is, in turn, closely dependent on the ingenuity and inventiveness of the software industry which drives the digitisation process.

The value of information is closely related to its delivery. Thus all industries and business processes that are 'information critical' — and hence the whole media industry — are among the first to feel the competitive opportunities and consequences of digitisation. Hence, too the coining of the phrase 'information superhighway' to describe a fibre-optic or satellite-based communication channell or the 'superhighway', the principal defining component of which is information.

Symptomatic of the magnitude of the transition is the way in which the giant international media and communications companies are jockeying for position to ensure their corporate survival. Telecoms companies, originators of intellectual assets, broadcasters, hardware manufacturers and software developers are rethinking the rules of the game. Indicative of this process is the spate of mergers, acquisitions and joint ventures as industries hedge their strategic bets. Often, surprisingly, such partnerships arise between two competing companies. This has given rise to the phenomenon of 'co-opetition', the cooperation amongst erstwhile competitors who realise that they have more to gain from collaboration than from sustaining their respective competitive positions.

Thus all sorts of unlikely alliances have been entered into as competitors enter the strange world where it is better to kiss the enemy rather than to spite the corporate face. Controllers of communication channels seek alliances with content producers, entertainment companies with broadcast transmission networks, cable television companies with hardware companies, consumer electronics firms with Internet software providers, and telephone companies with information companies. Electronic commerce and the multimedia revolution are driving the computing and telecommunications worlds into ever-closer contact, forcing two industries with traditionally different histories and cultures into both competition and cooperation. Hence the pervasiveness of the concept of 'convergence', or even collision, in describing the current re-shaping of the economy.

Industries that in the past were quite separate and distinct will experience increasing waves of acquisitions, mergers, joint ventures, and vertical or horizontal integration at the end of the 1990s and beyond the millennium. Convergence will occur at an accelerating pace, simultaneously driven by market, regulatory and technological developments. It will be facilitated by the development of broadband communications and, together with spin-off products and services, it will become the major stimulus to growth for the western economies into the twenty-first century.

Digitisation, the technology at the heart of the electronic revolution, will have a profound effect on all our lives. It will also transform the very nature of business itself. It will affect how we communicate with our customers; how business-to-business transactions are shaped; how supply chain management is organised; which products and services are offered; how alliances are conceived; which assets are regarded as valuable; and, the kind of corporate culture which a driven world demands.

Success in a digital world hinges on re-inventing business for the electronic age. As the electronic marketplace flattens, the competitive landscape of traditional commerce will change out of all recognition. This, then, is a fully-fledged revolution, similar in scope and impact to the industrial revolution of the nineteenth century. We are white-water rafting to an, as yet, unknown digital destination.

Chapter 2

Paradigm Shift

Digitisation, the technology at the heart of the electronic revolution, will have a profound effect on our business lives. It will influence how we communicate with our customers and how business-to-business transactions are shaped; how supply chain management is organised; which products and services are offered; how alliances are conceived; which assets are regarded as valuable; and the kind of corporate culture which such a driven world demands. In the process many of the business paradigms with which we are familiar will dissolve and, in time, new paradigms appear to take their place. By early in the twenty-first century whole new categories of business will have been created and others have faded away.

We are at the beginning of this transitionary phase, this move from the industrial, or post-industrial, society to the new digital age and the knowledge-based society. The traditional business landscape will change out of all recognition over the next twenty-five years in ways that, at the moment, we can only just begin to discern. To understand the dynamics of this transition we need to look at the way in which digitisation is redefining business structures. We also need to re-assess the very nature of business processes themselves. More profoundly still, we need to examine the structure and nature of work itself, and thus the implications of this transition for the shape of our corporate being and for the very nature of our economic identity.

RE-INVENTING CORPORATE STRUCTURES

Corporate structures have warped almost out of all recognition in the last fifteen years. Two trends have underpinned this corporate metamorphosis. First, the trend away from nationally defined business, towards globally defined business. Second, the structural re-engineering of all businesses, leading to a new downsized and streamlined existence.

Increasingly large corporations operate across the globe. They are no longer constrained geographically and defined within a national boundary. Moreover, the terms 'multinational' and 'international' no longer accurately define the nature of such corporations for they have transcended the confines of a 'nation' and thus the concept of 'nationality' entirely. They are global and they mean global business.

The Shrink-Wrapped World

Cheap and efficient communication networks allow global companies to locate their different business functions in different geographical territories as they see fit. Thus R&D could be located in Tampere, component manufacture or product development in Taiwan and assembly and warehousing in Toulouse. How would we know whether this was a Finnish company, a Taiwanese company or a French company? It is, of course, all and none of these. The glue which holds it together is its corporate identity and its shared values, most strongly represented perhaps in its brand identity. This doesn't mean though that cultural differences can be ignored and the world treated as an undifferentiated mass market. Much strategic advantage derives from corporate sensitivities honed to local markets.

A globalised company is one no longer dominated by a national headquarters with international presences merely a clone of the 'parent' company. The concept is not one of hierarchy, which the terminology 'headquarters' suggests, but rather one of flattened network structures – web-like infrastructures. In order to capture the essence of being global, companies have to build their identity and their intelligence on a number of inter-related levels. They have to be multi-dimensional and able to respond quickly to changes in the competitive environment. This calls for flatter organisations based on alliances and relationships both within the organisation and outside it. Competitive global advantage will go to companies who have the intellectual capacity to grasp the changing nature of the structure of markets and the potential of international enterprise, and to determine where their lucrative market niches lie.

In his book, *The End of the Nation State*, Kenichi Ohmae outlines his thesis of an economically borderless world.[30] If a company operates out of Taiwan, Thailand, France, Mexico and the USA, under whose jurisdiction does it reside? Furthermore, if its customers purchase its goods over the Internet, in which jurisdiction, or jurisdictions, do these transactions occur and in which currency will they be transacted? Ohmae talks about businesses being 'nationality-less' and global businesses being held together by shared values – and of industry, investment, individuals and information flowing relatively unimpeded across national boundaries. He also identifies the catalysts underpinning these changes: global communications, major market deregulation, and relatively cheap transportation. He thus refers to national boundaries as being '[economic] building block concepts appropriate to the nineteenth century'. The clear implication is that they are inappropriate for the last decade of the twentieth century and even more inappropriate for the twenty-first century.

Globalisation not only affects the structure and operation of any one particular company and its relationship to any one country, it also affects the speed at which competitive change occurs. While the great technological inventions of the nineteenth century – the railways, the steamships, the transatlantic telegraph cables – were possibly far more revolutionary than those of the late twentieth century – satellite links, the Internet, nanotechnology – the impact of the latter is arguably more immediate and more comprehensive.

Electronic communication is relatively cheap. It is also instant. In the nineteenth century, internationalisation was driven mainly by falling transportation costs, whereas now, in the late twentieth century, globalisation is being driven by plunging communication costs. This means much deeper international integration is possible. It also means that the process of disseminating information, analysing it, making decisions based on it and implementing these decisions is accelerated beyond recognition. Competition has become more rigorous and the competitive environment far more pressured and volatile. At any moment the whole nature and locus of the game can change and we will have flipped into a new paradigm almost without knowing it. Clearly one of the key survival skills in the twenty-first century will be coping with constant change and this applies not only at a global level but at a very local level as well.

This trend towards globalisation has not been the only corporate force at work. There has been an equally powerful trend towards shinkage in the body corporatė, and it has affected all companies. Whichever term you wish to use – re-engineering, flattening, downsizing, rationalising or re-aligning – major corporate re-structuring has been evident over the last decade.

This corporate shrinkage has been driven by a number of factors. These include first the continuing displacement of labour by technology; second, government policy favouring private enterprise over public ownership; and third, the culture and objectives of business, which have become focused on maximising profit and optimising short-term financial performance. In the process of shrinking themselves companies have outsourced a great deal of non-core business and thus developed a mass of sub-structures and supply chain alliances.

These developments are now overlaid by another dimension: the impact of digital technology. Digital technology is accelerating one of the key drivers of globalisation and global trading – the immediate and equitable accessibility of information. In addition to flattening, downsizing, re-engineering and re-alignment, we now have re-invention. Re-invention smacks of an altogether more fundamental configuration. It is not just about the rejigging of the mission statement, the melting away of a layer of management or the outsourcing of non-core functions. This is about rebirth, a totally new fabrication, a new embodiment – in short, reincarnation.

Success in a digital world hinges on re-inventing business for the electronic age. As the electronic marketplace flattens, the competitive landscape of traditional commerce will change out of all recognition. When many of the functions of supply and distribution can be achieved electronically, suddenly the whole structure of business and the value chain has to be reassessed. If you can distribute your product or service electronically, what then of warehouse charges, wholesaler margins and retailer mark-ups? If you can market your services to 40 million people – as on the Internet – at the same cost as marketing to 1,000 people, what then of traditional economies of scale? If you can save yourself the printing and mailing costs of 10 million catalogues, as in a traditional international mail order business, for the cost of an Internet site, then what of all that physical transportation to hundreds of countries worldwide? With the introduction of automated cash dispensers, the branch network of the high-street had undergone some shrinkage. This though will bear no comparison with the dramatic shrinkage of the banks' physical infrastructure which will occur with the introduction of digital cash and electronic banking. The result will be shrinkage of anorexic proportions.

Re-invention will not only mean the radical restructuring of existing businesses and industry structures, it will mean the generation of entirely new categories of business and the fading away of others. The case studies in Chapter 5 show how this process has begun. The digital revolution will soon be fully-fledged, similar in scope and impact to the industrial revolution of the nineteenth century. At the moment we can only see the faintest outline of the transformation which will occur, but this is no reason to ignore it. Indeed, quite the opposite. There is every reason to embrace it.

Small is Perfectly Formed

In the recent past, a prerequisite for being global was being big, but electronic communications in general, and the Internet in particular, have changed all this. The underlying ethos of the Internet was to create a free, and freely accessible, global community-based communications forum. Though this freedom is now compromised by financial prerequisites – Internet access charges – it always was compromised, in practice, by the necessity for access to technology. What has not changed though, is the egalitarian paradigm which underpins representation on the Web. Whether you are a business of one or a firm of 100,000, you will still have one Web site address, be indexed with equal sophistication by the same search engines, and be instantaneously accessible whether your customer is in Tiananmen, Tampere or Toronto. It is therefore both a humbling and an enhancing technology.

There is another dimension to this egalitarianism. Digital technology is a perfect medium for the communication of ideas. Intellectual assets are the source of wealth in any knowledge-based society. Moreover, they are enhanced in value by access to ideas and sources of inspiration, by enriched communication with colleagues, and by opportunities for reflection and diversion. Thus there is a close correlation between enhancing the source of wealth in a knowledge-based society and promoting communication. Instant, global communication may create problems of volume, of cyber-babble and of information overload, but if rigorously pared and contained, it will provide a conduit for inspiration and cross-fertilisation. Its unique value lies in its spontaneity, its informality and its borderless nature. It is boundary blind.

Individuals and researchers from anywhere on the globe can instantly trade ideas and the fruits of their intellectual endeavour. Whether these are embedded in e-mail, tossed into a video confer-ence with virtual delegates from Thailand, Poland and Canada, or, in the future, beamed by satellite technology into a microprocessor embedded in your watch, they will arrive instantaneously none the less. The days when the stolid establishment might thwart the genius of a John Harrison (seventeenth-century inventor of the chronometer) or of a Frank Whittle (twentieth-century inventor of the jet engine) are not, alas, entirely gone. However, elec-tronic communications do give latter-day innovators like them another conduit through which to circumvent the heavy hand of prejudice.

For those companies who will camp in the heartland of the knowledge society, being small may present substantial advantages. First, it lends itself to creative conviviality. In a knowledge society, where intellectual creativity is central to asset development, then to attract excellent intellectual artisans you have to provide a working environment which is creative, fun and congenial. Not only do creative content-makers tend to prefer close-knit teams to big business behemoths, but companies, like jazz bands, find it difficult to improvise with more than nine or ten members. A network of project teams provides the kind of infrastructure which promotes both improvisation and inventiveness.

Second, being small lends itself to adaptability and this, in a mercilessly competitive and rapidly changing world, is a key corporate asset. This is especially true where innovation, enterprise and intellectual assets, together with versatility and flexibility, are paramount.

Take, for example, the media industry. In conventional media, feature films or television for instance, an analysis of possible audience reactions is now regularly conducted prior to the start of production. However, once the film or programme is made there is little that can be done to alter it radically in response to audience reaction. Based on the reaction of focus groups, a film's ending may be changed, scenes edited or selected scenes may be shot afresh – the film may even be re-launched in a different country under a different title if it 'bombs' in the first country of release – but essentially we are talking about minimalism when it comes to alteration.

Not so in new media where there is no real concept of a finished product in the conventional sense. It is more a question of a constantly evolving product. When news is updated every fifteen minutes, or an entertainment product recreated every month, how convincing is it to talk of one complete, irreversibly final product? Because the product is under a constant process of evolution, there is a continuing sense of immediacy about it. It generates a more intimate rapport with its audience, forcing producers to listen more attentively to that audience and become more reactive. The management challenge lies in optimising this process, on the fly and in real time.

Thus the culture in new media is very different from that in traditional media. In the latter, artists and executives know absolutely the context in which they are operating. Moreover, traditional media is more static, more bounded and final. There is no such assurance in new media. New media requires you to be quite deliberately pragmatic. You are driven not only by content but also, and firmly, by technology. There is a sense of continuous motion in the industry which is at once invigorating and intimidating. Just keeping abreast of the technology becomes a demanding task in its own right.

While the need for such rapid adaptability is most obvious in the industries on the leading edge of new technology, other industry sectors will soon feel the impact, for such speed of change demands flexible organisations. Hierarchical organisations are out. Web-like organisations are in. In the same way that we talk about distributed computing, so also we can talk about distributed companies within one organisation. Survival depends on the ability to respond quickly to changes in the environment, whether those changes are technological, competitor or consumer led. In such a marketplace, sluggish, hierarchical organisations will struggle.

The New Malleability

In the digital age, re-engineering will cease to be an event; it will become a process. Swift corporate re-invention will become a necessary core competence. At the forefront of the digital revolution, the computer companies intuitively know this better than most. The title of the book by Intel CEO, Andy Groves, *Only the Paranoid Survive*, conveys the flavour of this necessity for constant re-assessment.[31] For leaders in this industry, the Bill Gates (Microsoft), the Larry Ellisons (Oracle), John Malones (TCI), the Louis Gerstners (IBM), the Edward McCrackens (Silicon Graphics) and the Eckhard Pfeiffers (Compaq) of this world, it is not just an occasional re-assessment of the competitive terrain which provides them with their success – constant vigilance is required. Some would call it a continuing, and deep-seated, paranoia or a state of constant orange alert.

Only the Paranoid Survive is a primer on how to cope with the 'strategic inflection points' which occur when the fundamental nature of a business changes and prompts dramatic changes in fortune. When a strategic inflection point has been reached a company is forced to dig deep into its psychic reserves. It will either rise or fall, depending on its corporate ability to adapt to challenge, but it will never be the same again.

Any CEO in the new media industry whose constitution is in the least delicate would never have survived the competitive rigours of the last ten years – and this doesn't only go for individuals, but for the corporate body itself. Whether we're talking about the computer industry, the television industry, the publishing industry or the telecommunications industry, it is clear that wide oscillations in fortune are endemic. Symptomatic of the uncertainty, turmoil and strategic re-positioning which multimedia has spawned are the waves of mergers, acquisitions and alliances: witness Disney's acquisition of Capital Cities/ABC, Time Warner's of Turner Broadcasting Systems and the creation of Cable & Wireless Communications and BT/MCI's Concert.

Moreover, we only have to look at the rapid rise of the cable industry in the States and the UK, and its unnerving capacity to unseat the conventional terrestrial industry, to see the effects of complacency – well, relatively speaking of course. Meanwhile, even the mighty Microsoft was caught out with the rise of the Internet and obliged to relaunch its Microsoft Network (MSN) service. While Rupert Murdoch's Delphi Internet service has pressed the self-destruct button, Murdoch's intent to corner the digital set-top market worldwide has grown apace. Another paradigmatic shift has occurred and another wave of paranoia is set in motion.

Perhaps the most dramatic and best documented challenge from nowhere was Netscape's Navigator software which still dominates about 65 to 70 per cent of the browser market. As short a time ago as the spring of 1995 Netscape was a relatively unknown software company, having announced its first products in September 1994. However, by August 1995 and its $2 billion flotation on the American stock market, it was planning to pitch itself against Microsoft, the biggest player in the industry. A David and Goliath story writ large – and one which continues.

All this raises the interesting conundrum that big may be a necessary condition of global success, but it may also sow the seeds of its own dysfunctionality. Unless a corporation can turn on its heel, at the drop of a hat, then it may have acquired for itself a core incompetence. As the dynamics of the industry continue to fluctuate wildly, the large corporates become even more vulnerable to the challenges from the nobodies from nowhere. It is rather disconcerting to think, as Andy Grove does, that 'business success contains the seeds of its own destruction' because the firm that enjoys the greatest success with one approach always finds it hardest to change.

RE-ASSESSING BUSINESS PROCESSES

Businesses are going to have to adjust to a corporate presence both in the real world, as it has always been, and increasingly in the virtual world.

We are familiar with the way in which digital technology, or more colloquially IT (information technology), has invaded the workplace. Regardless of the industry sector, computerised technology has to a lesser or greater extent altered the tools of our trade. Whether we are in graphic design, architecture, retailing, financial services, manufacturing, transport or biotechnology, the computer as business tool has become omnipresent. However, unbeknown to most of us, whatever computer we interact with, either as producer, servicer or customer, we leave a digital trail. As transactions are automated so they are digitally recorded, and as digital storage space is very cheap and ultra compact, this is easy, cheap, convenient and automatic. Thus, stored away in the recesses of a computer memory, or computers strewn all over the globe, is information about a myriad individual business transactions and business processes. Whether the information is about storage levels of components, customer purchase patterns, frequency levels of certain financial transactions, the identity of prospective customers, or the programmed mechanical actions of a robot, it is being used to tailor the processes, products and services of business. Over the recent past, managers have become adept at analysing this information to improve both business efficiency and business effectiveness.

Virtual Migrations

So far, so familiar, but the technological development which has taken us beyond purely the application of IT to the processes and products of business is the Internet. That global network of computers which enables us to communicate instantly, electronically and cheaply with anyone, virtually anywhere in the world, has been the catalyst to the creation of a new business paradigm. It provides new arenas within which to create business value; it plays tricks with the conventional business wisdom of economies of scale and scope; it provides new avenues down which to meet our customers; and it overturns conventional economic thinking about the scarcity and consumption of resources.

Since the early 1990s, companies have been experimenting with the possibilities which the Internet has opened up for global trade and commerce. While it was initially conceived as a non-commercial application, the Internet has subsequently been colonised – some would say hijacked – by business. The reasons for this colonisation are compelling. Companies have approached the possibilities of the Internet in two principal ways: first, as a way of adding value to their existing business processes in the physical world; second, as a way of complementing or relocating some or indeed all of their business functions out of the physical world and into the virtual world.

The initial and most familiar business development route in

cyberspace is route one, adding value. A commercial presence in cyberspace – most typically a Web site – not only provides a promotional tool for your physical products and services, it can also strengthen brand integrity and reach new market segments. So, whether the company is Federal Express providing its customers with a means to track their packages as they travel from their pickup point to their destination anywhere on the globe; Polygram providing a comprehensive catalogue of its artists and products, samples of its latest releases, and a search facility for locating its dealers; Bass Breweries promoting its Carling Black Label with an online information service for football fans and discussion forums on sporting issues; or Kellogg, the manufacturers of breakfast cereal, offering daily breakfast e-mails featuring the latest news, these corporate identities in cyberspace are primarily about enhancing brand image and adding value.

However, some companies have gone beyond adding value. They have relocated, either in whole or in part, certain of their business functions in cyberspace. While the process of manufacturing remains emphatically in the real world, and probably always will, the R&D, marketing and distribution functions have found a convivial and cost-effective niche in cyberspace. The production of media assets or products – newspapers, magazines, television programmes etc – is, and will increasingly be, affected by digitisation because many of the key tools of the trade – cameras, studios, laptop word processors etc. – are themselves digitally defined. Similarly, and quintessentially, the same holds true for software.

The way in which a whole business function could migrate to the Internet overnight was illustrated most dramatically in 1995 by the American company, Netscape Communications. It showed the ease with which a paradigm steeped in the accoutrements of the industrial revolution – factories, warehouses, physical distribution, shelf space – could be blown away in one breath. The company achieved this by distributing over 12 million copies of its Netscape Navigator in so-called beta test form, free over the Net, to anyone willing to try it out and report on critical bugs. Not only did this provide a zero cost worldwide distribution mechanism for the company and its software product, it also provided a cadre of computer software users who were willing to test out the software in return for a zero cost copy. Additionally, manufacturing costs were zero. Not for Netscape an international chain of dealers, resellers and stockists offering shelf-space visibility and taking margins of 15 per cent or more. Moreover, in an incredibly short space of time the company had seeded a new medium and even unnerved Microsoft, 'the' giant of the software industry.

All this does not necessarily mean that physical distribution, and its associated cost structures, will be eliminated overnight. What it does mean is a greater variety in modes of distribution, and also that executives will become skilled in creating value in both the physical world and the virtual world. Managing two interacting value-adding processes in the two mutually dependent realms poses new conceptual and tactical challenges. Competitive advantage will go to those executives who understand the differences and the interplay between these two value chains and thus comprehend the strategic issues facing their company.

Being Short-Chained

It doesn't stop here, for strategic developments go beyond just migrating business value or business function. Now entire businesses and indeed industry segments may be, and are being, subverted by the principles which underpin commerce in the electronic world.

A rather unappealing term has found its way into our digital vocabulary. It is the term 'disintermediation'. Evidently it has sacrificed beauty for exactitude, but ugly or no, it connotes a powerful new business phenomenon. This has particularly poignant consequences for intermediaries or agents in the value chain. It spells the elimination of middle distribution channels – or at least the physical intermediaries – for they will be 'melted down' and 'secreted away' under the double impact of digitisation and compression technology.

Traditionally they have acted as a necessary facilitator in the distribution of the 'stuff' of commerce – goods and services – but they have also acted as buffers, building barriers between the originator and consumer of a product or service. That intermediary in the value chain has earned his or her percentage by virtue of the value they have added to the total transaction. However, if, as in an electronic world, that intermediary value can be automated then the agent in the physical world can effectively be regarded as uneconomical or rendered redundant, or both.

Whether you are in the travel agency business, the insurance business, the banking business, the publishing business or the employment agency business, disintermediation will surely affect you. Adapt or die must be the new mantra. Why, for example, squeeze ink on to dead trees – one of the key processes in traditional publishing – when you can make the same intellectual property available electronically, and globally, for a relatively negligible cost? Digital delivery is not the panacea for all business ills – far from it – and there are still very sound reasons why newspapers, magazines and books like this provide unique value in their current physical form, but publishers, like all other producers in the real world, must also explore the possibilities of cyberspace and decide how to augment their business value in that domain. If they don't, surely someone else will.

All kinds of producers are asking the critical question: how can the necessity for granting distributors a percentage of the profits be transcended using the Internet? Customers are also asking this question. They are querying the added-value traditionally claimed by, for example, travel agents, insurance agents, and employment agencies. What real value do estate agents offer a vendor for the percentage they charge? By their nature, estate agents exist to connect sellers with buyers and landlords with tenants because these parties are unable to reach each other economically or effectively. As Ray Hammond puts it in his book *Digital Business*: 'In theory, agents offer professional advice about marketing properties, supply local information and act as a useful "cut out" in negotiations, but does this value need to have a high-street presence and a national chain of agency branches?'[32]

If the answer to this is no, then why should I as a customer pay for all those expensive overheads? Why not deal direct with the seller or buyer online via an electronic agent? Possibly the human contact injects warmth into the process of buying and selling property, but is it worth the agent's commission? If I had the option of shortlisting properties online in my chosen area, in my price bracket and complying to my preferred locations, then walking around them in 3-D virtual reality as a prelude to physically viewing the short-listed properties, might I not do so? Clearly such a service also costs money but, and this is the crucial but, it has eliminated the need for costly physical assets. It can also easily, and at no additional cost, market the property to prospective buyers whether they be in Perth, Penrith, Paris or Patagonia, or indeed all in the same city. According to the organisers of the real estate Connect 97 conference in San Francisco, 'buying a house in the US could be paper-free in two to three years'. There is a proviso though. 'Standard forms for electronic house purchase need to be developed, and a secure funds transfer mechanism found. We need a secure infrastructure with encrypted signatures.'[33] Undoubtedly though, such security will arrive.

If you, as a business, are liberated from the constraints of traditional overheads – tangible capital assets and the physicalities of supply and distribution – and have access to an immediate global marketplace, then the economics of market supply are radically altered. This means that whole new niche markets, hitherto too small, too dispersed and too fragmented, are now accessible and ripe for economic development.

This is particularly apparent in the tour business. You can now promote painting vacations in the Camargue, vineyard vacations in Bordeaux or architectural tours in Italy from your Web site. Anyone, anywhere in the world, at any time of the day, can now access this promotional information. Moreover, shortly, they will also be able to sample the ambience of such a vacation in 3-D virtual reality, confirm their booking when they've made their choice, and transact the process of payment over the Net. The cost of creating such specialist sites will be minute compared to the conventional costs of reaching such a specialist market. This will allow new entrepreneurs with an intuitive understanding of the electronic marketplace to offer quality tours at much lower prices than those which are traditionally marketed. Moreover, the degree of customisation possible will also be far greater.

The challenge of disintermediation will affect not only the travel and estate agency businesses but indeed all businesses which derive their income from being an intermediary in the value chain. Their whole physical *raison d'être* is now being challenged by the new electronic entrepreneurs, and from two angles. They will not only need to emulate the offerings of these new entrepreneurs, but they will also need to figure out how they can offset the costs of their physical assets, costs which their purely electronic competitors do not carry. It is clear that in such an environment only those companies which move quickly to the new electronic model, or embody an artful combination of the old and the new, will survive and thrive.

RE-DEFINING CORPORATE ASSETS

By definition, sustainable value resides in assets. In the nineteenth century and the early part of the twentieth century, business assets were manifestly tangible. This made their quantification, their location, their accountability and their valuation relatively straightforward. As David Potter, Group Chief Executive, Guinness Mahon Holdings, observed in his presentation to the *Financial Times* Broadcasting and New Media conference in February 1996, in terms of the great technological developments of the nineteenth century, the issues facing bankers were relatively easy, since they involved traditional fixed assets – hardware such as cables, iron and steel. He noted that such tangible assets have cashflows, residual values and definable costs which make for straightforward valuations. Although hardware remains a key element of the new digital industry, there is a new and equally important dimension – intellectual added value.

Invisible Assets

It is not only bankers, investment analysts and financiers who find the valuation of intellectual assets difficult, it is also governments. Customs declaration forms, tax return forms and company reports are still driven by a paradigm that belongs to a very physical and very tangible world. This fails to recognise, for example, that the value of a laptop resides in the software assets and intellectual property which are subsumed within it and not in its tangible exterior. Because microprocessors are routinely embedded in everyday objects, intangible inputs account for an increasingly significant percentage of the value of the product. As an indication of this, it is estimated that the value of America's stock of intangible investment – research and development, education and training – overtook the value of its physical capital stock during the 1980s.[34]

Charles Goldfinger, an economic consultant, argues that the shift from material goods to intangibles is the defining feature of the new digital economy. The fashionable talk is about the 'weightless' or 'dematerialised' economy. As production has shifted from steel, heavy copper wire and vacuum tubes to microprocessors, fine fibre-optic cables and transistors, and as services have increased their share of the total, output has become lighter and less visible. America's output, measured in tonnes, is barely any heavier now than it was a hundred years ago, even though the real GDP (gross domestic product) by value has increased twenty-fold. As production becomes lighter, it also gets easier to move. The average weight of a real dollar's worth of American export is now less than half that in 1970.[35]

Not only does value increasingly reside in invisible, intellectual assets rather than visible land or capital assets, but the central defining process in the value chain itself – production – is increasingly in the form of intangibles. Production here is based on the exploitation of ideas rather than material things. A production base centred on ideas can be extremely lean physically. As inventors, writers, artists and artisans know, the mining of the mind is a capital-lite process. It requires little material fabrication, little real estate. It does not rely on shipping lanes, on containers, on motorways, on warehouses or rail networks; it relies on communication: of ideas, of inspiration, of information, of collegiality, and of cultural imperatives.

A 1996 report noted that more than half of total GDP in the rich economies is now knowledge-based, including industries such as telecommunications, computers, software, pharmaceuticals, education and television.[36] Moreover, the high-tech industries have almost doubled their share of manufacturing output over the past two decades to around 25 per cent, and knowledge-intensive services are growing even faster. Hence the rise of 'knowledge workers' whose primary economic or market value lies not in their superior physical power nor their sophisticated tactile skills but in their cerebral ability.

The difficulty for the economist is that such intellectual assets, and the knowledge-based society which leads out from it, seem to defy the basic economic principal of scarcity. Knowledge is not scarce in the traditional sense. It does not diminish with use. Quite the contrary, it tends to proliferate and, curiously, to augment its value. Concepts such as depreciation and amortisation are not relevant in a knowledge-based economy, for knowledge is, as economists term it, 'infinitely expandable' and 'non-rival' in consumption. However much you use it, it is not used up or consumed. It is a sustainable, environmentally friendly resource. Indeed digital 'goods' can be replicated cheaply and consumed over and over again, their quality and viability undiminished. What is scarce in the new economy is the ability to apply knowledge and to generate an understanding of our business environment. This is where real competitive advantage lies. In future then the economies that perform the best will be those that develop and manage their knowledge assets more effectively.

The agricultural revolution and the industrial revolution were both embedded in, and embodied by, the physical world. While the industrial revolution ushered in mechanisation and urbanisation, the information revolution ushers in digitisation and globalisation. The key to opening the digital age is to understand how critical the intellectual asset is to competitive advantage. While intellectual capability has always been the main source of long-term economic growth, it is now also the mainspring of corporate survival.

Intellectual Capital

This relocation of business assets out of the physical world of machines and into the intellectual world of the knowledge worker has profound consequences for business, for the economy and, indeed, for society as a whole. These consequences have primarily three dimensions: first, economic mobility and thus the increasingly transient nature of employee loyalty; second, the knowledge workers' increased negotiating power because they are no longer 'workers' or 'labourers' in the conventional sense; and third, the knowledge workers' enhanced role in strategy formulation. Linked to all of these is the central question of business ownership. To understand these consequences we need to consider briefly some of their historical precedents.

Writing in the middle of the nineteenth century, Karl Marx noted that the industrial worker, unlike the artisans, crofters or smallholders of earlier eras, no longer owned the tools of their trade or the product of their labour: hence his coining of the phrase the 'alienation of labour'. The Enclosure Laws of the seventeenth and eighteenth centuries had effectively disenfranchised smallholders and crofters from ownership of the land which they tilled and later, with the industrial revolution, ownership of the factories and means of production migrated to those in a position to raise finance and invest in manufacturing assets – the so-called capitalists and entrepreneurs. Workers, and particularly those in factories, became 'hired hands': skilled in varying degrees, but hired hands none the less. Prior to the rise of the trade union movement at the end of the nineteenth century, their involvement in management decisions and their negotiating power was essentially negligible. Ownership, power and influence resided with the 'capitalists' and not with the 'workers', thus defining a new bifurcation in economic relations.

With the rise of trade unionism in the early twentieth century, coupled in Britain with widescale nationalisation in the 1940s and 1950s, the balance of ownership began to move out of the private and into the public domain. Come the 1980s, that pendulum had begun to swing in the opposite direction, in Britain at least. Ownership patterns began to resemble those of the mid nineteenth century, with the transport industries, the communications industries, the energy industries, and even social services migrating into the private domain. In short, come the 1990s, we see that all the industries and services critical to economic wealth are again privately owned.

This time, though, much of the value of a business resides not in its physical assets but in its intellectual capital and, critically, while people can be 'rented', they cannot be owned. Certain industries – aviation, transport, real estate, car manufacture – still require, and always will require, large, expensive machines and factories in which the key defining asset of the industry is manufactured. Investment in such machinery and capital assets will largely be by a limited number of people who have the means to raise the capital required and who are willing to take the risks associated with this form of capitalisation. However, in the age of intellectual capital, the most valuable parts of many jobs or assignments require professional or intellectual capital – the shrewd application of a body of knowledge to a business situation or a client's concerns. So far from being alienated from the tools of their trade, knowledge workers are intimately associated with them. Such workers bring not only their bodies to work, if indeed they need to do this, but more importantly their minds.

So, in a knowledge-based company where, say, 90 per cent of the value of the company resides in the intellectual assets of its knowledge workers, who owns these assets? While some of the value in a knowledge-based company can be harnessed and codified in patents, standards, codes of practice, databases and operating technologies, much of it resides in the intellectual capacity of its employees. As Thomas Stewart notes: 'A fundamental paradox lies at the heart of the Information Age organisation: at the same time that employers have weakened the ties of job security and loyalty; they more than ever depend on human capital.'[37] They are also doubly vulnerable in the sense that the most valuable employees are also the most mobile and, all other things being equal, most likely to migrate to other business opportunities. They take with them of course their intellectual powers – that is, part of the company assets. This puts a new spin on the concept of the 'brain-drain'.

Thomas Stewart suggests that organisations can help create bonds of ownership in both implicit and explicit ways. He cites two: fostering interdisciplinary teams and intellectual communities; and offering employees stock ownership. The first route encourages the sharing of intellectual assets and thus maximises the company's corporate gain from the input of any one individual. Also, because interdisciplinary thinking and small, dynamic 'think groups' spawn innovation and cross-fertilisation, everyone gains. Offering employees ownership in a company, like the co-operatives and mutual societies of the nineteenth century, not only spreads risk, it also provides employees with a stake in the fortunes of the company. Thus, it is in the employees' self-interest to maximise the prosperity of the company by staying wedded to it, as they gain directly by participation in its wealth. Says Michael Brown, CFO at Microsoft: 'Employee ownership is a profound example of how the Information Age has changed the nature of the corporation.'[38]

As ownership becomes communal, so necessarily do control and company direction – in a word, strategy. In his article, 'Strategy as Revolution', Gary Hamel cites deregulation, technological upheaval, globalisation and social change as the factors which are, at the end of the twentieth century, challenging the old industrial oligarchies of the past. Indeed, he sees such oligarchies, embodied in hierarchy and privilege, as a key strategic disadvantage: 'the bottleneck is at the top of the bottle'.[39] Where, he asks, are you likely to find people with the least diversity of experience, the largest investment in the past, and the greatest reverence for industrial dogma? It is at senior management level. Who are least likely to be living close to the future, and most likely to be furthest from the customer? The answer is, again, senior management. For traditionally, with honourable exceptions, it is senior management who have been the least likely to search for insight and ideas throughout the corporation, preferring by and large to exchange views within their own, necessarily incestuous, circle.

Such a narrow view is unlikely to gain competitive advantage in a business environment where survival depends on being constantly willing to challenge convention. As Hamel observes: 'Never has the world been more hospitable to industrial revolutionaries and more hostile to industry incumbents . . . It would be sad to conclude that a company can fully exploit the emotional and intellectual energy of a revolutionary only if he or she succeeds in navigating the tortuous route to the top.'

This democratisation of strategy-making demands a whole new mindset and a whole new paradigmatic shift in the concept of participation. The corporation can no longer afford to ignore the inspiration, the ideas, and the innovative capacity of its workforce, not least because, increasingly, they are the company's principle assets. As new ideas do not necessarily live within the borders of existing intellectual domains, so business innovation does not necessarily live within the boundaries of existing business models. This means that the milieu of enterprise in the twenty-first century must embrace some very anti-establishment thinking. Cultivating lateral thinking, idiosyncrasy and diversity will be a key leadership skill of the future as will attracting, valuing, nurturing and retaining talent. The mutual respect and the democratic nature of participation which this requires will mean that the businesses of tomorrow will live more by the precepts of partnership than by the precepts of hierarchy.

The Knowledge Worker

In the new economic age which the digital revolution will usher in, the roles of employees and employers will undergo a similar transformation to that in both the agricultural revolution and the industrial revolution. Indeed, it is already happening.

The pervasive development of technology has given rise to two key consequences. First, technology has replaced labour in the manufacturing process: this has happened in a far more complete way than could ever have been envisaged in the industrial revolution. Second, the pervasiveness of this technology has underpinned the move towards globalisation and highly competitive corporate environments. This in turn has placed increasing pressure on corporate executives to maximise efficiency and thus corporate profitability, at least in the short-term. As we have seen, the net consequence of both these market drivers has been the shrinking of the manufacturing base and the flattening of the corporate structure.

Thus, in the last ten years we have seen not only, in old-fashioned parlance, blue-collar workers but also white-collar workers displaced and dislodged from the corporate structure. This has led to (a) the prevalence of freelance or contract workers, (b) the rise of work discontinuities as the norm and (c) the creation of a core of 'permanent' corporate workers. Both groups, freelance and permanent, are under increasing pressure in the workplace, but for different reasons.

Many surplus white-collar workers have gone home to start their own businesses, as financial advisers, graphic designers, publishers, craft workers, software developers, editors, or management consultants. For the most part, they have done this not because they wish to, but because they have had to. They have had self-sufficiency thrust upon them. Silicon has changed everything. Robots have replaced muscle power; electronic surveillance has replaced human observers; menu-driven messaging and electronic system controls have replaced live operators. According to Don Peppers and Martha Rogers, we are being transformed by technology into a hunting-gathering society where 'silicon weapons' search out ideas and images, and workers 'forage' for services stooping to collect 'low-hanging fruit'.[40] He observes that we will all have to forage for ourselves, but we will not all eat well.

Like all revolutions before it, this transformation is not painless. Both for individuals and corporations it carries an element of anguish and dislocation. The manifestation of that pain was neatly expressed in the feature film, *Falling Down*, produced in 1992 and directed by Joel Schumacher. Here Michael Douglas plays the key character, William Foster or 'D-Fens', who, under duress from divorce, nihilism and the anguish of contemporary life, goes AWOL. There is a poignant moment in the film where D-Fens gazes in incomprehension at a fellow human being who is being 'moved on' for peacefully protesting against his modern-day predicament, his being 'not economically viable'.

As artists have always known, the work of freelance, self-employed or contract workers tends to be project driven. Contract workers move from idea to idea, project to project or contract to contract. Typically, work consists of either 'feasts' or 'famines'. The project workers' nirvana is to have continuous, digestible chunks of satisfying, remunerative work. Inevitably, though, there are discontinuities in the flow of work and thus in cashflow. In the same way as government departments still assume the accoutrements of sovereignty, though this is slowly dissolving, corporate financial institutions still typically assume an earnings pattern which belongs to the industrial or post-industrial era – that is, an even continuity of earnings and progressive salary increases. However, we know that it is not continuity of income that belongs to the digital age, but discontinuous earnings and oscillating salaries. But both nation states and the corporate institutions which underpin the assumptions of statehood are beginning to grapple with the consequences of a shrink-wrapped world and an information-rich environment.

Not only have the rhythms of work and the loyalties of the self-employed changed, those of the employed have changed also. The competitive pressures to be efficient and effective, and to appear thus, have increased on the slimmed down core of corporate workers. Here the pressures of performance are equally high and the threat of redundancy or non-renewal of contract hovers constantly on the horizon. No one is immune. The speed and accessibility of physical transportation and electronic communications have increased social mobility. With shorter-term contracts, higher mobility and greater instability, the corporate worker is perhaps no longer a core worker. His or her loyalty, understandably and in many senses rightly, increasingly belongs to himself or herself and not to the corporation, for the latter is no longer the repository of reliable stability.

While it seems that the constrained influence of trade unions and the dispersal of employees into individual or small entrepreneurial units has led to the waning of most workers' negotiating power, equally the individual negotiating power of the star employees or the gifted contract worker may be enhanced. Depending on the scarcity of their knowledge, the demand for it in the marketplace, the skill with which they can deploy it and the shrewdness with which they can market themselves, there will be rich pickings for such star workers. Moreover, with modern communications, they can market their skill and make it available instantly and globally. They can globe-trot their intellectual expertise. This makes them far more valuable than a century ago when they could only market their wares to those people they could physically meet.

What will matter in the digital economy is not whether you are located near critical physical resources, but whether you are located near critical electronic resources. It is of little value, now, to be located near large towns, motorways or a railway line. What is important is to be connected to optic fibre cabling and thus to the world of electronic communications. When people can exchange information electronically and video-conference globally, there is no economic need to meet physically. While the industrial revolution centralised the workforce, the digital revolution will reverse the process, scattering us to a pre-industrial configuration. So, geography will become far less relevant in defining where we work. Whether we operate from a garden hut in the Camargue or an office block in Los Angeles, it will make no economic difference.

These changes will, of course, not leave our social fabric untouched. Work is so essential to our identity, to our well-being, to our financial capabilities and thus to our economic independence that whenever it is under transformation then so are we. No one really knows what our society will look like at the end of this technological journey. Maybe it will be a meritocracy or maybe an aristocracy defined by intelligence quotients. What *is* certain is that, whether the knowledge worker (for that is now what we mostly are) is a lone hunter or a member of a marauding corporate herd, financial reward and economic viability will reside with those most adept, most nimble, most inventive and most shrewd at investing their cerebral capital.

Chapter 3

The Morphing Business

This chapter explores the contours of two industries. Both are well-established, with established traditions; both are being significantly affected by digital technology and both are visibly metamorphosing (or morphing as the jargon has it) under its influence.

With a tradition stretching back over centuries, the banking industry, characterised by branches, proprietary products and backroom operations, is being directly and deeply affected by the impact of new technology. Meanwhile, in the broadcasting industry, producers are beginning to experiment not only with digital production, editing and transmission but also with integrating programme research and audience communication into one digital domain. Both industries – banking and broadcasting – realise that the nature of their relationship with their customers and audience will change. Also under transformation is the nature of their competitors, for in this digital era competition will increasingly come from outside the traditional boundaries of an industry.

Digitisation is raising challenges to both industries in a more fundamental way than either has experienced before for the process of digitisation has sparked a series of what Andy Groves refers to as 'strategic inflection points'. Each industry then has to face changes to the fundamental nature of its business and has to find a competitive way of coping with dramatic changes in fortune. Both are forced to work harder to define their own turf and to map out their territory in the new digital terrain, and both will have to dig down into their psychic reserves and find a way to square the legacy of the past with the promise of the future.

DIGITAL BROADCASTING

The rise of technologies based on digitisation and compression has profoundly affected the fortunes of the broadcasting industry, for these technologies have provided a springboard from which all the multimedia and multichannel developments of the 1990s have been launched. Moreover, superimposed on digitisation and compression technologies have been the forces of industry deregulation and globalisation. In combination, these have created a highly competitive and digitally-based environment which now fundamentally affects the culture and direction of the broadcasting industry, both in the UK and worldwide.

Digitisation has affected the nature of production processes in broadcasting, and thus the shape of traditional broadcasting jobs, and the capacity of the transmission technology. It is also a catalyst for an altogether more profound change – over the next fifteen years broadcasting will be plunged into a fully digital milieu, where its traditional role and position will have to be re-negotiated and competed for far more vigorously than has been necessary, or perhaps even desirable, in the past.

Making an Impression

Excluding the development of the Internet for a moment, it is clear that digital technology has affected the broadcasting industry in two critical ways: first in the digitisation and miniaturisation of camera and editing equipment and, second, in the current move from analogue to digital broadcasting, that is, the digitisation of programme transmission. While the adoption of digital technology in the production process has been driven primarily by the need to increase efficiency, the revolution in transmission has occurred as a result of two key developments: the deregulation of the television industry in many European countries allowing the launch of more channels, and the emergence of digital transmission and encryption technology.

While the imperatives of lower production costs are perhaps more immediately apparent in the 'new' channels – cable and satellite stations – where production teams increasingly operate as a multiskilled unit equipped with digital camcorders and computer-based editing gear, the drive to achieve even greater efficiencies in the terrestrial broadcasting networks is also apparent.

In terms of production equipment, there used to be a substantial gap between the mass market for amateur and semi-professional equipment and the niche market for professional broadcasting equipment. However, the introduction of new digital recording formats has enabled the gap in quality between equipment used for broadcast television and the vastly less expensive equipment designed for the consumer market to be all but closed. As David Thomas notes, 'That will have an effect on the television business at least as significant as that of the Leica 35mm camera on photo-journalism in the 1930s.'[41]

The old distinction between broadcast television and non-broadcast video no longer holds. For example, camcorder equipment used to be the preserve of short 'amateur' video programmes, pre-eminently *Video Diaries* broadcast by the BBC, but we are now beginning to see segments of other broadcast programmes shot with hand-held camcorder equipment. Although Hi-8 camcorders sparked this development, it is really newer equipment like Sony's digital DVCam (digital video) format, which offers picture quality to rival BetaSP, which is the true catalyst in this process.

As an appropriate production technology, digital camcorder equipment comes into its own in documentary and factual-based programming, for example, in situations where a conventional camera crew would be an intrusion. Indeed this is one area in which the BBC wishes to encourage 'smart production'. The BBC's pioneering Smart Production initiative has supported several 'smart pilots' including the BBC1 daytime series *Morning Surgery* and the late night BBC2 broadcast, *Soho Stories*, while digital camcorders are now being used for inserts on *Watchdog* and *The Holiday Programme*. Meanwhile the 1997 series, *How Buildings Learn*, was shot entirely on DV format and edited on MCXpress workstations, an online editing system from Avid. Digital graphics have been used for some time both in programme production and in promotional inserts, and now virtual reality software is being used to simulate studio facades and Virtual Production Planner software for director training and planning purposes.

It is still, however, early days. Reduced though it may be, there is still a perceptible gap in quality between digital video camcorders and desktop PC editing facilities on the one hand and traditional production equipment on the other. Certainly prime-time programming for Carlton, for instance, will not be shot on a digital camcorder in the near future, nor the next BBC classical drama. Digital camcorders and computer-based editing gear do not necessarily improve programme quality. In fact, some fear exactly the opposite. Doubtless there will be some disasters for this is in the nature of innovation, but there will be a great deal that is fresh and challenging.

Thus, digital technology will have a profound effect on the production process albeit, in the short term, at the corners of the industry. Over the next ten to fifteen years it will have a far greater impact as digitisation seeps into all aspects of production in a much more comprehensive way. As happened when Channel One employed video journalists – essentially each is a production team of one – digitisation will reduce the size of camera crews, it will alter the skill levels and mix required, and, indeed, it will alter the dynamics of the industry. With the cost of digitally producing a pilot programme coming within the financial limits of the independent producer, and a multiplicity of channels looking for material to fill their schedules, the power base in the industry will begin to migrate away from the commissioning editors and broadcasters and towards the programme makers.

As David Thomas observes: 'The changes generated by digital television will not happen at once. Some programmes may hardly change at all, for the television industry has a very large investment in existing equipment to worry about, and considerable emotional investment in its assumptions about the ownership of skills.'[42]

The industry has, however, attached less emotional investment to transmission technology, as distinct from the tools of production and the cultural imperatives of programming. Industry deregulation and the emergence of digital transmission technology have allowed many more channels to be transmitted in a given frequency band than does conventional analogue transmission. In combination these developments, one regulatory, the other technological, will give rise to the creation of hundreds, if not eventually thousands, of television channels carrying programmes and services via terrestrial, cable and satellite television. UK terrestrial broadcasters plan about thirty-five new channels to be launched by the autumn of 1998, while digital satellite, through British Sky Broadcasting (BSkyB) is planning the launch of 200-plus channels in spring 1998. The technology behind digital satellite, like digital cable, allows more channels than digital terrestrial.

This suddenly ushers in the prospect of more than 250 additional television channels by the autumn of 1998, compared with a total of about 50 today – that is, about 300 in all, a six-fold increase within a six-month period in 1998. These, however, may not be channels as we conventiohally understand them but, rather, distribution channels for delivering conventional programmes in different ways. New programmes may indeed be broadcast on these new channels, but it is highly probable that the majority of programmes will be either (a) archived programmes as originally broadcast, or (b) live events broadcast over a number of 'channels' offering different camera angles, or (c) the relay transmission of the same movie over different channels, effectively delivering near video-on-demand, or (d) new interactive services that, initially anyway, sit some way between Teletext and the Internet in terms of content and technical sophistication.

The paradox of digital television is that while it should be a golden opportunity to genuinely widen viewer choice, it is arguably being driven by the desire of the UK's leading media groups to increase their grip on TV distribution outlets and pay-TV revenue. Pay-TV – charging for channels – has revolutionised the economics of television – new technology and deregulation allow TV companies to raise revenues directly from viewers. That frees the commercial industry from its traditional dependence on advertising which has shackled its growth. It also allows channels with small audiences, incapable of attracting much advertising, to be profitable. However, it also makes it a lot more difficult to be profitable as a niche provider without charging a premium price. Willingness to pay will have a ceiling. With high fixed costs and fixed viewing time, new methods of distribution are, arguably, more of a challenge than a solution.

Like the Internet and multimedia CDs, whether digital television takes off depends on the compelling nature of the product, how well it functions, and the price point at which it is offered to the market. It also depends on its simplicity and its ergonomic ease of access, for it is not audience demand which is driving digital developments in the broadcasting industry, but technology itself and the competitive appetites of the industry players. Moreover, it is highly unlikely that 'passive' linear viewing over a small select number of channels will disappear completely. In fact, ironically, the surfeit of channels available may whet the viewers' appetite for exactly the opposite: highly selective 'passive' viewing of original compelling programmes which no amount of interactive glitz or archived programme choice, however heavily marketed, can quench.

Casting on the Net

Broadcasters are beginning to experiment not only with digital production, editing and transmission, but also with integrating programme research, audience communication, production and transmission into one digital domain. This experimentation process was illustrated very well by the thinking behind Granada's Talk TV channel. Though eventually defeated by the economics of the marketplace, the channel was a courageous attempt to fuse television with communications technology. While most broadcasters now have a sophisticated Internet presence with e-mail audience links and 'added value' complementary programme information on the Web, plus, in some cases, related CD-ROM publishing activities, the thinking behind Talk TV was to push the digital boat out even further. It was visionary enough to see the potential of channel links with a network of cybercafés combining satellite, videophone and Internet access, encouraging audience participation by phone-ins, fax-ins, videophone connections and electronic mail.

Similarly, in 1997, the BBC World Service began experimenting with how a programme might be researched, produced, edited and transmitted entirely using digital and Internet technology. This experiment included, for example, editing interviews on a laptop PC and sending them to an ftp (file transfer protocol) site over the Internet, and eventually transmitting the final edited programme, again over the Internet. Limited bandwidth and quality loss with live Net transmission mean that, in the short term anyway, Internet transmission is not a viable distribution channel for BBC radio. However, other elements in the digital mix, like the Digital Audio Voice Editor (DAVE2000) software and the electronic news production system (ENPS), which can be accessed by any programme office in the BBC and digitally holds all correspondents' dispatches, are viable.

Aside from the application of digital technology to the production and distribution of television programmes in the last twenty-four months, we have also seen experimentation with interactive television on the Net. The Internet was originally designed to be 'driven' by the user. It is a highly interactive medium. However with the explosion of Web sites we have also witnessed a reversal of the original Internet paradigm and moved, in Web-speak, from a 'pull' technology to a 'push' technology, that is, from individuals 'pulling content' from the Internet to companies 'pushing content' on the Net. Hence the rise in 1996 of companies like PointCast, Marimba, BackWeb Technologies, Intermind and DataChannel. Terms like 'channel' and 'casting' now jostle with the more familiar Web terms like 'site' and 'homepage'. Indeed the Web has taken on some of the accoutrements of television as conventionally understood.

When Channel Cyberia was launched in May 1996, it described itself as the world's first scheduled 24-hour Internet channel and, somewhat like a conventional TV channel, it hosts programmes from independent content providers whose revenue is calculated as a percentage of channel revenue. A similar model applies to the latest Microsoft online service, MSN (Microsoft Service Network), which was launched in the UK in November 1996. MSN invites programme and 'episodics' proposals from independent television producers. It hopes to attract audiences by making the online experience televisual, with a move towards scheduling its programming to capture the idea of a shared event, but with all the interactivity that the Web can supply. The company plans to spend $1 billion over the next three years on content for MSN, of which 'double digit millions of pounds' will be spent in the UK, according to Steve Billinger, executive producer of MSN.[43] While viewing figures and budgets are low by terrestrial and traditional broadcasting standards, in comparison with some of the niche cable stations MSN's programme budgets and viewing figures are significant.

While these are not television channels in the way we understand them, they are attempting to 'broadcast' a schedule of both live and recorded events for a global audience. While the Internet in its current technological state does not have anything like the two-way bandwidth which will provide the instantaneous transmission of television-quality video images, it does have many of the elements of a broadcasting, or more accurately narrowcasting, industry. The concept is there, the interactivity is there, a business model is developing and an audience is congregating.

International Data Corporation (IDC) analyst, Frank Gens, anticipated that together with Internet commerce servers, Web site analysis/management, Internet application servers, and Java-based developments tools – content and software 'push' technologies would be 'hot' in 1997.[44] He also anticipated that the number of Web users worldwide would double to 68 million. Future growth beyond 1997 will come from the increasing market penetration of multimedia PCs and, crucially, from Internet access via the TV and, of course, as a result of compelling content. It is, however, still an embryonic 'netcasting' medium with return on investment a lengthy process and a significant risk. Thus, as with multimedia publishing, Internet publishers must become increasingly resourceful and inventive if they wish to see their digital investments generating significant returns in the short term.

Broadcasters including Channel 4, BBC, BSkyB, Flextech and Granada, are embracing the creative and business challenges of this new medium. In many senses the growing presence of the broadcasting industry on the Internet signals its firm move into the digital age. A digital multichannel environment mimics many of the attributes of the Internet, and indeed also of CD-ROMs, themselves now increasingly linked to the Net. With digital television and the Internet potentially available from the same 'WebTV', the dividing line between the two technologies must surely begin to dissolve.

Digital Mutations

The nature of recent joint ventures, mergers and acquisitions illustrates the degree to which the future of the broadcasting and the computing industries are interwoven. The omens are that eventually both industries will converge on one digital domain. Already these industries sit digital cheek by digital jowl. Unpredictably enough, it may be the television interface rather than the computer interface which opens up the Internet to a mass market.

In the autumn of 1996, Larry Ellison, CEO of Oracle, the US technology company, officially launched Oracle's new Network Computer in Paris. As the name suggests, the network computer, or NC, is designed primarily to access information and facilities stored centrally. It is a scaled-down, scooped-out PC providing shrink-wrapped access to centrally-held resources including the Internet.

Earlier in the autumn came the announcement that leading multimedia software developer Macromedia was to license its Shockwave Director software to Oracle as part of the reference design of the NC operating system. This transfer of Internet hardware and software from the PC to the TV can also be seen at work in Netscape's autumn 1996 announcement of its new company Navio Communications, which will produce a version of Netscape's Web browser software, Navigator, for non-PC platforms including televisions.

Hot on the heel of these developments, the electronic and entertainment group Philips Electronics launched its Magnvox WebTV in the USA at the beginning of October. The launch of the television 'box' was the first fruit of a deal with WebTV, a Silicon Valley firm that is developing Internet on TV technology. In autumn 1996, Microsoft formed a strategic partnership with WebTV and the two companies announced their intention to collaborate on technologies for delivering Internet content to television. WebTV will integrate aspects of Microsoft's Internet Explorer browser into a future release of its WebTV browser system. In April 1997, the relationship developed further when Microsoft announced its acquisition of WebTV.

Microsoft's acquisition is a mark of the company's determination to play a leading role in the convergence of personal computing, online services and consumer electronics in advance of the launch of digital television in the USA in 1998. Significantly, Microsoft has also proposed technical standards for linking the Internet and digital television which have been backed by more than twelve television manufacturers, consumer electronics companies and Internet software companies.

At the 1997 National Association of Broadcasters convention in Las Vegas, Microsoft, Intel and Compaq outlined their intent to 'work cooperatively' with the broadcasting and cable TV industries to 'realise the full potential' of digital TV across a range of PCs, hybrid PC/TVs and digital TV appliances. The companies set forth technical recommendations, based initially on a subset of the Advanced Television Systems Committee (ATSC) specifications, that they claim would accelerate the transition to digital television in the States.

Indeed, Microsoft envisages a broad range of consumer electronic devices – from Internet telephones to hand-held Internet terminals – for which it aims to provide software. Not insignificantly, Microsoft's Internet Explorer browser – developed in the face of Netscape's competition – and Windows CE operating system for pocket computers will be incorporated in WebTV products.

It is not hard to fathom the lure of television for companies like Microsoft. Currently, home computers have a penetration of about one-third of American homes, and merely 10 per cent of homes in Europe and Japan. Television, however, has found its way into 98 per cent of US homes and is similarly ubiquitous in the UK. It is predicted that television access to the Internet will expand rapidly from about 50,000 US households in 1996 to over 20 million by 2000, according to Jupiter Communications, a US market research group. With the migration of the Internet to the television and the launch of digital television in 1998, it may be that the battle for audience share will then be far more comprehensive, far more demanding and far more rigorous than has so far been envisaged by the broadcasting and telecommunication industries, or indeed the computing industry itself.

CULTURAL TRANSITIONS

One of the key implications for traditional broadcasters in this new digital world is that the nature of their relationship with their audience will change. This digital age demands a new mindset and attitude which places the audience at the centre of the broadcasting process. A multichannel environment and an Internet awash with thousands of sites means that not only will broadcasters have to compete more vigorously for their audience share, but also that they will have to compete with a range of new and diverse 'content and delivery mechanisms'.

According to Intel estimates, about 90 million PCs will be sold in 1997, compared with 100 million television sets. Within 18 months, the US chipmaker expects PC sales to overtake sales of TVs as the home PC becomes a consumer appliance – and, according to Price Waterhouse's 1997 Technology Forecast, young adults in the States, between the ages of 18 and 35, who previously spent an average of four hours a night watching television, are now devoting one of these hours to the Internet.

A *Financial Times* report states, 'It seems today's digital age consumers, especially the "wired" generation reared on e-mail, MTV, video game machines and, of course, the Internet, crave interaction, connection and unlimited choice.'[45] Changes in information delivery mechanisms are also expected to lead to changes

THE DIGITAL ENTERPRISE

in content, in order to exploit the full potential of new delivery
channels such as the Internet. 'Media will move away from being
for the masses towards being for the individual', according to a study
published by Dresdner Kleinwort Benson. 'This will manifest itself
as increasingly niche and tailored services.'[46]

There is no doubt that the interactive and immediate nature
of the Internet, and thus other digital arenas, has implications
for the relationship between the broadcaster, the narrowcaster,
the webcaster and the netcaster and their audience. Like other
artists in the new medium, Fred Stewart, an established American
novelist and writer for the Internet 'cyber' soap, *The East Village*,
feels invigorated by the challenge of the new. 'It's like Hollywood
in the 1910s and the television industry in the 1940s: there are no
rules. If anyone says they really know what they're doing then
they are either hypocrites or liars,' he says.[47] He was attracted to
writing for the company Marinex Multimedia which produces *The
East Village* because it represents 'a new and dynamic way to reach
an audience. The feedback is immediate.'

Digging Deep

The major impact of digitisation on broadcasting will be concertinaed into the next five years. During these 'cramming' years,
participants in the broadcasting industry will be invited to dig
deep into their skill reserves, to suck at the marrow of creativity,
to compose all manner of unlikely project teams and to develop
an ability to re-group at will. Doubtless the road will be scattered
with constraints – the most difficult deadlines, the tightest briefs,
the meanest budgets. Somehow a circle will have to be squared.

Together deregulation and new technology have had a profound
effect on the landscape of British broadcasting. From only three
UK terrestrial channels in 1980, there are now over forty cable and
satellite channels with about 200 digital satellite 'channels' due for
launch in 1998 and 35 digital terrestrial channels due for launch in
July 1998. However, the impact of digitisation goes far beyond the
'mere' multiplication of available channels. It is, in fact, beginning
to reshape the nature of the production process itself and to alter,
both subtly and profoundly, the way in which broadcasters interact
with their audiences.

The creation of The Internet Webcasting Association Europe

(IWA-Europe) in the summer of 1997 and the new types of skills being sought by traditional broadcasting organisations are indicators of the changing nature of the production process itself. According to an article which appeared in *New Media Age*, the aims of IWA-Europe are 'to promote the effective and efficient delivery of multimedia content over the Internet, through cable and satellite and other digital delivery networks.'[48] The IWA-Europe will be aimed at 'broadcast media, content developers and producers, Internet Service Providers, Internet technology companies, advertising agencies, communications firms, and educational and cultural organisations'. The juxtaposition of those content, communication and computing interests encapsulates the convergent nature of the industry dynamics.

In June 1997, BBC Worldwide, the commercial arm of the BBC, placed recruitment advertisements in the *Guardian* newspaper – nothing unusual about this, except that they appeared in the *Online* supplement of the newspaper and not in the *Media* supplement as would have been traditional. The reason is evident: the jobs advertised included Web Development Manager, Web Development Design Manager and Interactive Software Engineer. Qualifications required included 'an understanding of the latest web technologies'; 'experience with Unix and NT operating systems, and of using C++, J++, Perl and JavaScript'; 'an understanding of Systems Management, LANs, WANs and Servers'; and, 'a strong commitment to the BBC and the Web'. At the moment the BBC Worldwide 'Beeb' Web activities are but a very fine sliver of the BBC's total programming output, but these advertisements and the developments which give rise to them represent the thin edge of the Internet wedge in broadcasting. Should Internet access via the television take off, it will become increasingly difficult to tell where passivity ends and interactivity begins.

This array of new skills is giving rise to new team-working challenges. Doubtless challenges similar to those encountered at MSNBC – the cable and Internet news channel recently created by MSN (see case study in Chapter 5) – are also being encountered at, say, BBC News Online. Describing MSNBC as an 'unconventional media marriage', the journalist, Alicia Shepard points out how traditional journalists have left secure jobs at the *Wall Street Journal*, US News and World Report, ABC News, the Associated Press, CBS News and the *Los Angeles Times* to be part of 'a forward-looking experiment mixing network TV, cable and the Internet'. Rather than providing a familiar newsroom setting, MSNBC is:

> . . . a virtual Tower of Babel with its refugees from the worlds of print, television, radio and computers speaking in their own strikingly different languages . . . It's a land where writers are called 'content providers' and most journalists find themselves working next to people who think with a different part of the brain, to whom 'getting granular' means getting down to specific details.[49]

However, despite this new departure into digital terrain, it is the case that many, if not all, of the traditional broadcasting skills are required, and perhaps required more urgently, in the new broadcasting and media publishing environment. Traditional broadcasting skills are central to the concept of creativity in the new medium and established professionals are well-placed to demand high production values and to promote cross-fertilisation.

The new broadcasting world also demands a broader mindset and a wider appreciation of the concept of teamwork and of interactivity. In an article in *Broadcast*, the author refers to the interviewee's belief that producers will need to acquire three sets of skills in the new media world.[50] First, a new approach to programming: instead of leading viewers through a linear and re-packaged series of images and sound bites, producers will need to orchestrate viewing options. Second, a fresh approach to management: with programmes being made by individuals with diverse skills, project managers with an overall vision and managerial 'grip' on the project will become more important. And third: greater computer literacy. Quoting the producer Kevin Newport, the author also notes that a willingness to embrace the concepts, culture and assumptions which the computer world inhabits will become a *sine qua non* for survival.

Ironically, digital technology and multimedia will perhaps change the role of the producer least. Indeed, it may lead the producer back to the glory days of the producer as impresario. The production scheduling of a conventional programme and the consequent juggling of resources, talent and time constraints, is difficult enough, but the complexity of this process is compounded when further media elements and skills are combined as in multimedia. Thus, more than ever before, the producer becomes 'master of ceremonies' and 'juggler extraordinaire'. This role demands a talent for decision-making under duress; for tolerance, empathy, leadership and team motivation; and, for the 'grand vision' for the final product. In the transition phase to a multichannel digital environment, it will demand a particular understanding of the skills and creative insights which non-traditional team members, particularly those from a computing background, can bring to the production process.

By contrast, the role of the scheduler may soon pass into television history. The increasing irrelevance of programme scheduling, or transmission sequencing – for it will be superseded by programme 'orchestration' as a key broadcasting skill – points to this new approach to programming. As John Wyver noted in his TV21 article, 'With the viewer able to choose from a multitude of channels, the layout of any one of these will become increasingly irrelevant. Repetition of either programmes or programme forms (as with MTV) will become the norm. Scheduling as traditionally understood will join alchemy as an arcane art of interest only to historians.'51

Thus an understanding of and empathy with computing and computer programming and the mindset which underpins it will be a key broadcasting skill in the next five years. Critical, too, will be a new and deeper appreciation of the programme audience and a keener wish to develop audience rapport. Inevitably, as indicated by John Wyver, this means going beyond 'just' rapport and into a more shared programming-making process between the 'broadcaster' and the 'audience'. This, in turn, demands perhaps a less egotistic mindset and a greater willingness to invite audiences to participate in the very process of programme-making, an area traditionally regarded as sacrosanct by most broadcasters.

With Attitude

In his TV21 article John Wyver lays out a 'highly speculative' ten-point producer's survival guide. It illustrates well the differences in attitude and culture required in this new televisual arena. Though the article was written in 1994, the thinking behind it remains both valid and prescient. The ten-point guide reads as follows:

One, think publishing, not broadcasting; two, think selection, not schedules; three, think intelligent black box, not television;

four, think Internet, not ITV; five, think marketing, not advertising; six, think marketing, anyway; seven, think programs, not programmes; eight, viewers have the final cut, not producers; nine, think copying, not copyright, and finally, ten, above all, think attitude.

Honing in on point eight regarding the viewers' cut, he noted the following:

Whether or not software 'agents' become the predominant form of independent production in 2020, it is certain that viewing will be a far more dynamic and involving experience. Computer games, CD-ROMs, and today's crude forms of interactive television indicate some of the paths that this may take, and others will emerge in both factual and fictional television. Producers will have to respond to the way that viewers and users engage with the screen. Feedback will not be confined to responses by e- or ve-mail (although these will certainly mushroom), but will encompass the wholesale remaking of programmes.[52]

One of the most critical survival skills in broadcasting, as in all industries, will be an ability to remain innovative and flexible. Very hierarchical or bureaucratic organisations have the most difficulty with this as they nurture a culture that is not conducive to risk and experimentation. Without risk, experimentation and failure – for failure is an essential concomitant of success – the chances of corporate survival and prosperity decline rapidly. If everything is calibrated and quantified, the entrepreneurial necessity for some degree of creative space cannot be justified. Without some space, there is no room for growth – and without growth, there is no survival. If calibration is all, then enterprise is diminished.

In broadcasting, as in all industries, more and more 'strategic inflection points' will occur more frequently in the future. The skill is in the anticipation, in coping with the trauma and in riding the ambiguity. Adopting a formula or painting by numbers will never produce a Rembrandt, nor will it ensure corporate survival. In fact, it may very well obscure that essential lateral thinking which keeps an organisation nimble, alert, talented, energetic and dynamic. Thus the off-beat, the novel, the inventive, the unexpected, the shrewd, the savvy and the eccentric must be valued, particularly in those with a hand on the strategic tiller. In a world that is changing so quickly, an ability to re-invent oneself, to partner with an erstwhile competitor, to think the unthinkable, and to remain focused, will become at once altogether more difficult and more important.

BANKING MIGRATIONS

The last twenty years have seen radical changes in the financial services sector, a sector in which technology has been one of the most important drivers of change. In particular, information technology has had a significant impact on business processes, on customer services, on areas of competitive advantage and on the national branch structure. During the 1980s, the diffusion of IT through banking processes and the eventual ubiquity of automated cash dispensers led to the contraction and the rationalisation of the local branch network. The British banking union BIFU has recorded 120,000 job losses in the past six years.[53] These technologically-related pressures have been compounded by the impact of deregulation and the consequent spate of mergers, acquisitions and flotations. This shrinking process is destined to continue further as the banks and building societies seek to reposition their products in the new financial landscape and to realign themselves in a new and highly competitive world.

Deregulation and competitive pressures have resulted in an increase in the number, complexity and sophistication of financial products on offer, and in business diversification by most financial institutions. Thus banks no longer concentrate purely on cashflow, currency facilities, and high transactional activity. Equally, the building societies no longer focus solely on long-term investment facilities and mortgage lending. These days are gone, except for specific niche players. They have each diversified into insurance, pensions, investment products and estate agency activities. Moreover, certain of these functions are now being 'hi-jacked' by large companies in non-finance sectors which have a strong brand presence and a high marketplace visibility. For instance, Sainsbury, Safeway, Virgin and Marks and Spencer are now offering select banking facilities, insurance policies, pensions, and investment products.

Depending on how you look at it, the banking sector faces either another threat, or the possibility of a further opportunity. While electronic banking has been around for a decade or so, it has been limited in its application and based on proprietary software. The global ubiquity of the Internet entirely transcends the original parameters of electronic technology. Its rise is forcing the banks to encompass online banking in a far more comprehensive way than was thought possible, or even desirable, merely twenty-four months ago. With barriers to entry relatively low, and a global marketplace immediately available, all kinds of new financial entrepreneurs are 'setting up shop' on the Internet. All the big clearing banks, for example, recognise the threat posed to their traditional role as transaction intermediaries, where Internet service providers, software companies, hardware developers, retailers, telecoms and media companies might create infrastructures through which commerce is conducted.

From the customer's point of view it is, arguably, a small step from arranging financial services and transactions over the phone to arranging them personally and directly on a computer screen. Such access is under the individual's control, transcends the need for an intermediary (disintermediation) and is available 24 hours of the day, 365 days of the week, anywhere on the globe. It does, of course, demand a digital connection, a PC (or equivalent), Internet or private network access software, and a modem, but if all that is installed at home for other purposes, then why not use it for personal finance as well?

Jupiter Communications, a New York research firm, predicts that the US home banking market, for example, will grow to 18 million households by the year 2002 compared with 2.5 million in December 1996. By 2005, it estimates that 75 per cent of all homes in the USA will be practising some form of home banking from PCs and the number is expected to grow to 95 per cent by 2010. Given these predictions, it is not surprising that the banks are re-examining their core business, re-assessing their unique advantages and looking for ways of extending that advantage on to the Internet. In a sense they have had the migration to the Net thrust upon them. The challenge is to find ways of taming this new technology and the competitive pressures that surround it in order to sustain a viable banking business.

A Perfectly Placed Product

The innovative features of the Internet make it a particularly powerful medium for business communication and a novel marketplace for commercial trading. No physical goods need to change hands. Moreover, its immediacy, its appeal to high income earners, its relatively low cost entry point and its accessibility, make it particularly attractive to businesses in the financial services industry. Indeed, the Internet seems purpose-built for the precise needs of this industry.

Why? First is the very nature of the product. Financial services are quintessentially 'soft' goods. They are intangible except for 'old-fashioned' cash. Their very economic substance can be represented electronically and communicated digitally. Moreover, the information-rich nature of the products make them eminently suitable for online interrogation. While there are obstacles to growing the market – for example concerns about security, fraud, the lack of immediate ease of access and lengthy download times – it is also the case that many influential companies have a vested interest in removing exactly those obstacles.

Second is the desirability of the demographics from a profit point of view. There is a high positive correlation between the people who own computers and use the Internet with those who have relatively high levels of disposable income to invest in financial products. Moreover, a significant proportion of Internet users hold managerial and professional positions, and thus have influence over substantial business assets as well as the most lucrative personal assets. As experience of electronic banking in the States demonstrates, e-banking clients tend to be more affluent and are much sought after.

Third is the impact of electronic trading on transactional costs. *The Internet Banking Survey*, conducted by Booz·Allen and Hamilton, calculated the cost of the average payment transaction on the Internet to be an estimated 13 cents or less. According to the report, this compares with 26 cents for a personal computer banking service using the bank's own software, 54 cents for a phone banking service, and, one dollar eight cents for a bank branch transaction.[54] While less than 1 per cent of banking transactions are processed from home at the moment, these differentials and customer demand suggest that this will change radically over the next five years.

The Booz·Allen and Hamilton survey also showed that by the end of 1997 a projected 56 per cent of European banks aim to have a full Internet service, and revealed that by the turn of the century, more than 15 per cent of US households could have access to Internet banking. It further estimated that because these early adopters will largely be drawn from the upper income (and more profitable) groups, they will embody 30 per cent of the profits in the retail banking sector.

While the US banks may have led the exploration of electronic banking, the UK banks are also getting in on the act. In 1997, the Royal Bank of Scotland announced that it was setting up a full Internet banking facility; the Bank of Scotland that it was trialling Internet-based online banking; and Barclays Bank that it was launching its PC banking service with links to the Microsoft Money personal finance package. Other banks, including Midland, NatWest and Lloyds TSB, have also been active in exploring personal electronic banking services, though not all of these services are accessible via the Internet. Some, like Barclays, rely on proprietary systems based on special software and accessed by a private network. In the 1980s, when US banks, such as Citibank, and UK banks, such as the Bank of Scotland, pioneered online banking, this was standard. Now, with the spread of Internet standards, proprietary systems appear somewhat outmoded, but caution about the Internet is understandable if not also wise.

There are extant limitations to the Internet as an e-banking access route. It is still true that only a small proportion of PCs in European countries have Internet access. Barclays, which estimates that 35 per cent of its UK current account holders have a PC at home, believes only 800,000 of them have access to the Internet. Moreover, people are concerned about the security of financial transactions on a public network such as the Internet, and also response times are slow compared with proprietary software links. However, any edge that proprietary software enjoyed is being swiftly eroded. Internet usage is growing about 10 per cent a month in the UK (office and home), and, while it remains an issue, the security of transactions over the public Internet is improving as strong encryption becomes embedded in Internet browser software. Moreover, as Internet access rates increase, first with the introduction of the latest modems working at 56 kilobits per second (Kbps), and later with the adoption of technologies such as cable modems, speed will become less of an issue. However it will only be when security ceases to be a central issue, and Internet access is available to a mass market, that online banking will really begin to take off.

The Infrastructure Impact

These developments strongly suggest that retail financial services will find a convivial home on the electronic superhighway in the not-too-distant future. This, of course, raises considerable issues for financial institutions in terms of global competition, transnational business and territorial identity. Nearer to the heartland of its business, it also raises fundamental issues about how to balance the organisation's 'physical' existence with its 'virtual' existence, and thus how to redefine the unique contours of its business.

The traditional financial sectors, particularly retail banking and the building societies, have inherited extensive – and expensive – real estate: their nationwide branch networks. In addition to this very physical legacy, they have also inherited a firmly established array of business processes and a company culture which are premised on the actuality of the physical world. So, ironically, while the Internet offers these companies the opportunity to add a new low cost business channel to their operations, it also poses a threat to their market share as it neutralises so many of the traditional competitive advantages of having a nationwide branch network.

Furthermore, the traditional players have to absorb greater electronic start-up costs than new entrants, as they have to integrate their electronic presence with their existing, and extensive, physical presence. For a green field player starting an Internet bank from scratch, as did Security First Network Bank (see case study in Chapter 5) in October 1995, buying the software off-the-shelf is estimated to cost in the region of one million dollars – relatively speaking, hardly a high barrier to entry. For the established players, adding another transaction channel without reducing traditional channel costs merely adds to the existing overhead. It does not reduce it. Thus one of the key challenges for the banks and building societies lies in figuring out how to re-engineer and optimise their existing branch network.

A report by the accountancy and consulting firm, KPMG pointed to the radical changes in culture and style which banks will have to undergo in order to pull off competitive profits in this new and demanding electronic world.[55] It concludes that the titanic struggle for the loyalty of retail customers will be won by those who build the strongest personal relationships with individual customers. Nothing new here perhaps, however, the target is no longer necessarily volume business but, increasingly, a greater share of the personal finance business of the more affluent individuals. It is also about radical changes in style. The report notes that banks will have to come to terms with rapid changes in technology, the almost complete re-invention of management and decision-making structures and, above all, they need to become highly skilled at brand building and customer care. Consequently the technological, cultural, marketing and managerial challenges facing retail banking are immense.

Perhaps surprisingly, the KPMG report maintains that branch banking is not in terminal decline. Its findings say that while the role of the branch is expected to shrink, the branch network will continue to account for a significant volume of financial transactions. Branches, KPMG believes, will become the focus for building personal relationships with customers. Achieving this rapport depends in part on the replacement of the traditional hierarchical banking structure with local decision-making power and close-knit, web-like teams, for, as in all other industries, hierarchy spells delay and, increasingly, inflexibility and in the new competitive world of financial services, inflexibility and long deliberation spell corporate extinction.

SPACE INVADERS

While having to contend with the implications of technological developments, the traditional financial sector, characterised by branches, proprietary products and backroom operations, is also having to defend its competitive space against at least three groups of new players in the business.

First are the companies offering direct financial services – services which circumvent the need for a nationwide physical infrastructure by using only the telephone and mailing services to transact business with its customers: in a sense a precursor to electronic banking. Since First Direct pioneered phone banking, NatWest, Bank of Scotland, TSB, Save and Prosper and others have followed suit.

Banking executives realised that not only was phone banking a way of reducing costs, it was also considered, like ATMs, useful and convenient by consumers. In less than five years First Direct attracted more than a reported 500,000 customers with a growth rate of up to 10,000 customers a month. At the end of 1996 NatWest had around 540,000 customers using its phone banking services. Significantly, it also announced plans to cut 10,000 jobs in branches in the next four to five years.

The second group of new players comprises non-financial companies, primarily the big supermarkets – like Sainsbury, Safeway and Tesco – but also including other strong brands like Virgin and Marks and Spencer. An increasingly deregulated environment allows a different breed of business into the banking world. In 1997, first the Bank of Scotland linked up with Sainsbury, which obtained a banking licence in February of that year, then the Abbey National teamed up with Safeway and the Royal Bank of Scotland with Tesco to provide select in-store banking facilities. The Scottish banks – which have limited customer bases in England and therefore run less risk of cannibalising their own business – have pursued the strategy of 'co-opetition', that is, cooperation with a possible competitor. However, the larger English clearing banks, like National Westminster, (the original favoured Tesco partner), Barclays and Lloyds TSB, sense that the chances of cannibalism and marginalisation through possible 'co-opetition' with the supermarkets are not worth the possible financial gains.

Tesco launched its Visa credit card in July 1997, the first of a planned series of financial service products which are expected to include current accounts, mortgages and personal loans. As its partner, the Royal Bank of Scotland, owns Direct Line insurance, and Scottish Widows has a significant share in the Royal, so insurance and pensions will also be on the agenda. Royal Bank of Scotland Chief Executive, Dr George Mathewson, was quoted as saying that he expected the joint venture – known as Tesco Personal Finance – to contribute a substantial portion of the bank's annual profits.[56] The Royal has a 51 per cent stake in the project and expects to invest around £20 million.

The Bank of England which authorises new banks, raised a number of possible concerns about supermarket banks in its 1997 annual review of the banking sector. The Bank said it was important that customers should have a clear view of the ownership of a newly authorised bank, and showed some doubt about the compatibility of the supermarkets' management culture with that of banking. On the supermarkets' side, they run the risk of damaging their own brands and reducing customer loyalty by, for example, refusing credit to those they consider uncreditworthy.

Opinions vary as to whether supermarket banking poses a serious threat to traditional high street banks. However, they do seem to be treating competition from food stores with caution. NatWest's worries of undermining its own customer base caused a retreat from supporting Tesco's Clubcard Plus account. Tesco Personal Finance and Sainsbury's Bank keep overheads to a minimum by operating solely by telephone, and as a result are able to offer more competitive interest rates than traditional banks. Moreover, unlike the traditional banks which are shackled to fixed costs, from running branches through to the processing of cheques, the supermarkets have only to absorb the variable costs traditionally associated with sub-contracting in a host of other industries. Consequently they have more scope to sacrifice more profit margin than banks do on competing financial products.

Also, as observed by Professor David Llewellyn in a seminar on banking in the twenty-first century, the cause of concern is not necessarily that the supermarkets will snatch all the business. Rather the competitive damage will be wrought by the supermarkets cherry-picking the 'juicy bits'.[57] This implies that the real test of supermarket banking will be whether the stores can tap their captive market, make use of the detailed database revealed by customer shopping bills, and build on their brand image to cross-sell other financial products such as personal loans, personal equity plans (PEPs), pension plans, investment, mortgages and insurance policies.

The third area of competition to the supremacy of traditional banking is the growing trend towards electronic banking or e-banking. The growing standardisation and resilience of Internet protocols, robust encryption, and browser software, has ushered in a new commercial world which is electronically and globally based. This has opened up a new channel to market and a new playing field for the delivery of banking services. Unshackled by legacy systems, new entrants are challenging the traditionally conservative banking institutions in this new and largely untamed domain.

In both the States and Europe, the banking sector now realises how critical this competitive arena is to its future survival and prosperity. It is clearly in the banks' interests to find innovative ways of strategically re-positioning themselves in the marketplace. Strategic alliances with retailers and with technological companies are one response to this business re-think. Developing their own proprietary and/or Internet-based online banking service is another, as is entering an online banking consortium. Accordingly they have taken action. In the autumn of 1996, Louis Gerstner, chairman of IBM, and the CEOs of fifteen banks with 60 million depositors – including Banc One, Nations Bank and Bank of America – announced the creation of the Integrion Financial Network, a nationwide online banking network. Integrion can be reached by customers via IBM's network or the Internet online services, America Online or CompuServe. Through this consortium, the banks hope to preserve their brand image and achieve economies of scale for this complicated technological venture.

Some consider the reason behind Integrion to be mainly defensive, while the banks themselves see it as an essential step in maintaining their brand advantage and control over their own financial systems, instead of ceding that control to, for example, a supermarket chain or a technology company. Unlikely though it may at first appear, banking customers may develop more familiarity with the financial software package on their PC than with a 'distant' name which was their bank. If the interface with, or 'gateway' into, your financial services is not your local bank but your software package then the possibility that loyalties will begin to transfer are fairly high. In this context we can see how Intuit or Microsoft, with their Quicken or Money software packages for personal financial management, can provide the front end to a new Intuit or Microsoft bank. For not only can you download information from your banking statement and integrate it immediately into your personal financial records, but at some point you will also be able to cruise the Net in search of the best credit rates. In this scenario, the customer would have more of a 'relationship' with a personal finance program than with any single bank, and bank branches would go the way of the dinosaurs.

So, the traditional banking industry is faced with the challenge of a loss of share to each of these three sets of competitors. While in combination they may not sever a bank's ties with its retail customer base, they may weaken those ties, obscure brand value and steal much of the profits. Banks are therefore working hard to preclude this possibility and to preserve the value of their brand name. This will demand new management thinking and new company cultures. Two recent reports signal the technological and attitudinal changes sweeping through the banking industry in response to this challenge.

The first report, *The Information Superhighway and Retail Banking*, urged bankers to get involved in interactive electronic services before non-bank companies locked in a permanent competitive advantage.[58] The report warned that if banks spend too much time 'on the periphery of information superhighway changes, new competitors can enter and take market share from the banking industry'.

William S. Haraf, senior vice president of Bank America Corporation and chairman of the Institute Center for Banking Issues and Strategies, wrote in the foreword to the report: 'We will need to leverage our customer and transactional information and to position ourselves to play the role of the navigator . . . Finally, we must both protect and enhance our content and integrate our distribution channels with online delivery.' The underlying message, then, is that computer and communication advances are of critical strategic importance to bankers, and bankers ignore them at their peril. Conservative American analysts predict a doubling of Internet and commercial online users to 15 million US households by the year 2000.

The other report, *Retail Internet Banking*, was based on two surveys, one of the US market and one of the European market.[59] This survey found that Internet banking will almost certainly become a major fully-fledged distribution channel of banking services and products in Europe within the next three years, but in the short term Internet banking growth will be limited by technological developments, security concerns and consumer behaviours. However, in the longer term, Internet banking's low-cost structure and appeal to young affluent consumers will confront banks with a variety of strategic choices, including how to compete in this new environment, how to migrate their customer base and how to differentiate their services.

Thinking Strategically, Thinking Laterally

To summarise, the following five developments paint a picture to which a strategic response is required by all the players in the financial services industry: first, the impact of new technology, mergers and acquisitions on the building society and banking branch networks – that is, continuing shrinkage of the branch network and the realigning of business on the remaining network; second, the encroachment of the big supermarkets into the banking business, and thus their possible expansion into the lucrative bits of financial service products, including pensions, PEPs, investments, insurance and mortgage provision; third, non-traditional competitors with a strong brand – Marks and Spencer and Virgin for instance – entering the direct financial services market plus their possible expansion into banking; fourth, the movement of the banking industry online, both in the States and in Europe, and the development of associated collaborative ventures with computer and technology companies; and fifth, the innovative features of the Internet technology as a new business channel.

The position of the banks and building societies as significant players in the financial services industry is thus bound to be under pressure to change and to adapt to those combined challenges. It is not necessarily the impact of any one of those developments in particular which is potent, but more importantly, the new competitive landscape that is painted by a consideration of their combined effect. In order to respond to these challenges business leaders in the financial services need to consider how to achieve the following: sustain their market leadership; mesh a real and a virtual existence; cashflow innovation; create a compelling online presence, and sustain a coherent market presence.

If this seems like a demanding agenda, that's because it is. Although banking, like broadcasting, is at the heart of the digital revolution, these industries will not be alone in confronting these challenges. They will, however, be among the first. Digital technology, as we have seen, represents both a severe threat and an intoxicating opportunity for all businesses in the financial services and media industries. The executives know that the spoils of competition will go to those companies which can apply exactly that competitive mix of entrepreneurial flair, market expertise and business nouse which made them great in the physical world, successfully migrate those assets to the electronic world, and balance a competitive existence in both the real and the virtual worlds. This will be the key management challenge in those industries over the next ten years.

Chapter 4

Digital Titans

There have been many column centimetres devoted to a discussion of convergence: of technologies, of industries, of businesses, and of strategic interests. This is not without good reason, for in understanding the dynamics of this convergence we can begin to get a handle on its strategic implications; implications for the shape of business as a whole, for the sources of our future prosperity and for the architecture of the emerging global economy.

One of the most effective ways of approaching the subject of convergence is to illustrate it in action in a series of case studies. This chapter sets out to do that by charting the strategic course of three 'digital giants': Microsoft Corporation, News Corporation and British Telecommunications (BT). These companies, and the industries to which they belong, represent the three critical building blocks of the digital economy – computing, content and communications. Just as physical communications, mechanical technology and the factory system laid the foundations of the industrial economy in the nineteenth century, so electronic communications, digital technology and contracted intellectual assets are laying the foundations of the digital economy at the end of the twentieth century. In concert, computer technology, digitised content and electronic communications, large growth industries in their own right, will directly affect which businesses become dominant in the twenty-first century. Moreover, they will affect which become most central to local, regional and national economies and, indeed, the very way in which business is conducted and commerce plied.

Both Microsoft and News Corp. are intimately identified with their creators, respectively Bill Gates and Rupert Murdoch. Each has his hand closely on the corporate tiller, and can sustain repeated buffeting whatever the source whether it be vigorous competition, stringent government regulation, federal agency investigation, city analyst interrogation, attempted character assassination, the awesome fear of uncertainty or the psyche demands of high and continuing risk. Rupert Murdoch has been building his business for over forty-five years, Bill Gates for a 'mere' twenty-two. Both are regarded as digital titans, as corporate giants and by some as figures of awe or, contrariwise, as figures of strong distaste. Both are involved in digital technology and digital content in a big way, investing literally billions in their chosen growth paths. Murdoch started as a traditional owner of media assets and Gates as a developer of computer software, but both have grown closer in a business sense, particularly in the last five years, as Murdoch has expanded into digital satellite technology and Gates into the development of new media assets and creative technology.

By contrast, the telecommunications industry has never been as closely identified with one individual nor, indeed, so obviously dominated by one company. Until relatively recently most telecommunication companies were nationally-based, serving a regulated, and predominantly domestic, customer base, but with recent telecom deregulation in the UK and the USA, and with liberalisation on the horizon in continental Europe in 1998, the shape of the market is beginning to alter. The international alliances of America's AT&T and Japan's NTT, and Concert, the original venture between Britain's BT and America's MCI, signal the trend towards global expansion in this industry.

Superimposed on technological advance and deregulation has been the rise of the Internet. Whether this is finally delivered via our television screens or our computer screens, or more probably both, the telecoms industry is destined to play a highly significant role in the Net's development. And whether the final carrier of the information superhighway is a fibre optic cable or a satellite beam be sure that those industries with an interest in both, and thus the communications industry par excellence, will be central to the global chess game of digital connections.

MICROSOFT
Commanding Position

First we turn to Microsoft and the origins of its dominance in computer software. Microsoft was launched by Bill Gates and his partner, Paul Allen, in 1975. The negotiations between Microsoft and IBM at the end of the 1970s signalled the first of many masterstrokes by Microsoft. The combination of the MS-DOS operating system and the Intel processor which formed the heart of the IBM PC, launched in 1981, laid the foundations for the subsequent rapid growth of Microsoft to the point where it soon outpaced IBM – the big blue – itself. Moreover, Microsoft also struck comparable deals with IBM's early rivals like Compaq and Dell, before they could seek alternative software vendors, leading to Microsoft's MS-DOS becoming the *de facto* PC standard.

When Apple launched its Macintosh in the early 1980s, Microsoft copied the window-style on-screen display for its own generation of Windows software. If imitation is the sincerest form of flattery, then Apple should have regarded itself as highly flattered. By 1990 and the launch of Windows version 3.0, the capability and intuitive nature of the interface made it a serious competitor to Apple, though many regarded it as technically inferior. Those who witnessed the video tape format wars of the early 1980s, or the squariel versus the satellite dish battle of the early 1990s, know that superior quality confers no automatic rights to the mantle of industry standard. Much of Microsoft's success has been derived from its excellent marketing skills, its keen sense of business timing and its shrewd analysis of market dynamics. Arguably these skills have been more critical to its success than those associated with technological innovation and product sophistication.

Meanwhile, in terms of its applications software, Microsoft was making serious inroads into the competitive white space. Through exploitation of its software advantages, Microsoft began to outpace the competition, overtaking Lotus spreadsheet packages, WordPerfect word processing software and various other database packages in the market stakes. In time Microsoft reduced them to also-rans in terms of market share. So, by 1995, Microsoft's Excel spreadsheet software had captured 80 per cent of the world market, its Word package 70 per cent and Microsoft PowerPoint presentation software 75 per cent. This dominant position was further reinforced in the autumn of that year with the launch of Windows 95, a new, enhanced and empowered version of its operating software. Hardly coincidentally, in 1995 the company doubled its advertising budget to £150 million in support of a global branding campaign.

In 1995, with the new Windows 95 operating system, earnings surged by almost 50 per cent and profits hit $2.2 billion on sales of $8.6 billion. By 1996, Microsoft held a commanding position in the worldwide software stakes. The company had grown by about 30 per cent a year. About 87 per cent of all PC operating systems sold in 1996 were Microsoft Windows. Apple Computer's Macintosh operating system came a distant second with just over six per cent, while IBM's OS/2 achieved a share of just over two per cent. The picture was similar in the 'suites' market for packages of office applications programs. Microsoft Office was the market leader with an 84.5 per cent market share, by revenue, in the second quarter of 1996, according to Dataquest.[60] In the second place was IBM Lotus's SmartSuite package with 7.8 per cent of the market. Corel, which acquired the WordPerfect subsidiary of Novell, increased its share of the market rapidly, but still came in third with a 7.7 per cent share.

Thus, virtually single-handedly, Gates has shaped one of the world's largest industries. Between 1992 and 1996 Microsoft's shares almost quadrupled in value. This success is reflected in the personal wealth of Bill Gates, its Chairman and CEO. In September 1996, the company was valued at $75 billion with $8.7 billion turnover in annual sales. In February 1997 Bill Gates's holdings of over 140 million shares were worth $18 billion. Astoundingly this is more than the individual annual economic output of 106 countries. His wealth, valued at $28.8 billion, exceeded the national GDP of, for example, Nigeria ($27.9bn per year), Vietnam ($23.4bn), Ecuador ($17.9bn) and Iraq ($17.8bn).[61] This is no mean climb in twenty-two years.

The dominance of the Microsoft Windows operating system lies at the very core of Microsoft's power. In 1996 there were 20 million users of Windows 95 and 100 million users of Windows 3.1, the predecessor to the 95 version. The key to Microsoft's success in the software business is that it has linked its operating system, Windows, to its productivity applications, tools and network servers in a tight, interdependent chain. This enables it to make rather audacious moves. Thus, for example, eyeing online as the vanguard of interactive media's next generation, Microsoft built MSN, a proprietary online service and – creating serious aggro for competitors like America Online and CompuServe – announced that it would put the MSN registration icon on every Windows 95 desktop. Since Windows is the market leader, anyone in the chain from applications developers to hardware manufacturers and, increasingly, networked business systems, must continue to tie their product development plans to Microsoft's in order to remain relevant in the market.

Challenges from the Wings

However, all is not sweetness and light for Microsoft. It has had, and continues to have, serious challengers. One such is Netscape. The rapid rise of Netscape in 1996 undoubtedly unnerved the Microsoft executives. In early 1994 the company did not even exist, yet by December 1995 its market valuation exceeded $5 billion. Netscape had developed an Internet browser – Netscape Navigator – which provided a clean, intuitively convivial and highly accessible interface which enabled individuals to surf the Net easily, precisely and cleanly.

Gates had always stoutly maintained that Microsoft could never afford to be complacent because the nature of the industry permits new challenges to appear at any time, but here, Microsoft found it had misjudged the popularity and the momentum driving the Internet. It had been busily constructing its Microsoft Network online service based on non-Internet compatible proprietary software as a challenge to the 'big-timers' online – CompuServe, America Online and Prodigy.

Recognising its error, and the rise of Netscape to a dominant position in Internet browser software, Microsoft launched its offensive in the form of Microsoft Explorer as a rival to Netscape Navigator. Moreover, it has embedded this browser in its forthcoming Windows 98 revised operating system. As Microsoft supplies the operating system for 85 per cent of the world's PCs, this means that even supposing only 30 per cent of PC owners upgrade their operating system, then Explorer will automatically be installed in 25 per cent of PCs worldwide and come 'Explorer-ready'. No mean strategic achievement this. It is Microsoft's domination of the operating system market, and its sheer size and industry weight, which is enabling it to challenge Netscape's lead in the browser market so effectively.

Meanwhile, fleet-of-foot Netscape has re-focused its business emphasis away from the Internet browser market and on to the corporate intranet market. Netscape's president, Jim Barksdale, who has dismissed the browser wars as 'the current bloodsport in the popular press', says, 'The real money is in intranet software – that is where 80 per cent of our revenue comes from and we have always said this is going to be our main market.'[62] The American market research company, Zona Research, anticipates that intranet software sales will top $7.9 billion in 1998, compared with Internet sales of less than $2 billion.[63]

Microsoft however has no intention of leaving Netscape unchallenged in the intranet world. As an indication of its determination to penetrate this market and its awareness of the value of twinning with other established global brands, Microsoft announced its intention to develop global intranet services together with BT and MCI at the end of 1996. The new services which include information management tools, electronic mail systems, project collaboration tools, and powerful directory facilities, will be marketed worldwide by BT and MCI and offered by Concert, the existing BT and MCI joint venture global communications company.

Meanwhile Microsoft faces other challengers from other more established players. Not short of determination, enthusiasm or self-confidence, Oracle Chairman and CEO, Larry Ellison, has been attacking Microsoft's hegemony from a different angle. His is a software and hardware pincer movement. In May 1996, Ellison announced his endorsement of the network computer (NC) concept from more than fifty high-tech companies – computer and consumer electronics manufacturers, software companies, distributors, telephone companies and retailers. They included industry giants such as Sun Microsystems, Apple Computer, IBM and Netscape Communications.

He is championing the NC concept. This is a shrink-wrapped, scaled-down PC with its insides effectively scooped out: a 'thin client' connected to the Internet or a corporate server from which programs and applications are downloaded, as and when required. At a stroke, this concept neatly transcends the need for PCs as traditionally understood and thus for Microsoft software or Intel processors. Some critics of Intel have quipped that 'hyping the Intel chip is as absurd as selling a car by its exhaust'. Clearly Ellison thinks it is an exhausted concept. Tired of the rigours and complications of bloated software, Ellison reckons that what business hankers after is lightweight simplicity. This would trigger a shift in the centre of gravity in the computer industry from PCs running Microsoft software to NCs running Java-orientated software and Oracle database systems. Goodbye Mr Gates, hello Mr Ellison. Well, maybe.

Initially, and publicly at any rate, Bill Gates dismissed such an NC concept as impractical, misplaced and irrelevant. He has, however, subsequently quietly eaten his words. So much so, in fact, that later in 1996 Microsoft and Intel announced their joint plan to develop low-cost NetPCs, with leading manufacturers – including Compaq, Dell, Digital Equipment, Gateway 2000, Hewlett-Packard, Bell and Texas Instruments – similarly announcing their plans to manufacture such NetPCs. This constituted a direct response by the PC industry to the competitive challenge of NCs.

Moreover, in May 1997, Microsoft paid the firm Citrix around $100 million for its Win Frame software, which turns Microsoft's Windows NT server into a multi-user operating system. This means that a network server running Windows NT can download the operating system to multiple 'client' systems, whether they be PCs, NetPCs or low-cost Windows terminals, the latter of course simply being NCs in disguise. Clearly Bill Gates has an enviable knack of creating sustainable advantage from apparent mimicry.

Getting Netted

However, there was another unexpected challenger which definitely came from the wings. It was initially consigned a rather insignificant role by Microsoft and tidied away into a small strategic corner. It was, of course, the Internet. In 1994 and early 1995, Gates, like Murdoch, regarded this hyped upstart as a rather tactical development that had got too big for its strategic boots. Amazingly developments finally found both Murdoch and Gates in the unaccustomed position of being on the wrong foot.

In 1995 the high-profile success of the Internet and the Web, which are genetically coded to be agnostic about operating systems, threatened not only the relevance of proprietary online services like AOL, CompuServe or Microsoft Network online service, but also

Microsoft's entire model of market dominance. It provided, albeit in embryonic form, an alternative and attractive software platform. This realisation spawned Microsoft's Internet strategy, a complete corporate about-face, announced in December 1995.

The fear was that the Microsoft business might slowly be bled away by competitors who considered the Internet, not Windows, to be the platform for which they created and distributed their software. Microsoft had to find a way of embracing this loose cannon and surgically inserting it into its value-chain. Consequently, Microsoft announced early in 1996 that it would shut down the proprietary version of Microsoft Network (as was) and migrate it directly to the Web's non-proprietary HTML standards. This it did and re-launched it in the UK in November 1996 as version 2.0.

It also set about developing its own Internet browser software, Internet Explorer and embedding this into its Windows desktop. It thereby built Internet access into its entire existing suite of products, from applications to tools through to servers, going for a tight integration of its Internet browser software on the one hand and its multimedia and productivity applications such as its office software suite on the other.

In fact, this Internet access may eventually disappear from view entirely, effectively secreted away into Microsoft's existing interdependent chain of operating systems, applications and servers. This is the measure of its strategic importance. Towards the end of 1996 it was Bill Gates himself who noted that in the USA nearly 40 per cent of US homes had PCs and anticipated that in a couple of years virtually all would have Internet connections.

However, Gates's approach is not only to provide software access to the Internet but also to provide content for it, thus making a neat link between his Windows dominance and his rapidly expanding portfolio of digital media assets. As Gates sees it, digital technology is driving the media and software industries together. Both are brand-name businesses and benefit from economies of scale.

Thus apart from Internet-compatibility, the main distinguishing feature of the revamped MSN was an expansion of content. Microsoft introduced Expedia, an online travel booking service being jointly launched with American Express; Microsoft Investor, an investment management service for trading stocks online and tracking markets; The Plaza, an online shopping mall; and Sidewalks, an ambitious plan to offer a localised online city-specific entertainment listings and booking facilities, initially in the USA. Moreover, Microsoft is also signing up other content providers for privileged placement on its so-called active desktop, a part of its Internet Explorer version 4.0. The first such partner was Pointcast Inc. which carries channels from Time Warner Inc.'s CNN and many newspapers including the *Wall Street Journal*.

In order to extend its influence, Microsoft has developed a series of links with other developments which provide alternative distribution channels for MSN. Thus it has alliances with UUNet Technologies Inc., DirecTV Inc., MCI, AOL, CompuServe, Tele-Communications Inc. and Teledesic. For example, MCI, AOL and CompuServe have all agreed to bundle either Microsoft's Internet Explorer browser or portions of the Microsoft Network, or both, with software for their online services. Bill Gates is one of the major investors in Teledesic which is developing low-orbit satellite communication technology for inexpensive wireless global communication.

Obviously Microsoft has ambitions for MSN. The American consultancy and market research company, Jupiter Communications, predicts that Microsoft will at least achieve its short-term goal of doubling the number of subscribers to MSN during 1997.[64] Some commentators predict the growth rate of paying subscribers will triple, leaping from 1.5 million at the opening of 1997 to 4.5 million at the close. Like Murdoch and his satellite ventures, Microsoft says that it does not expect to make money from MSN in the medium-term. In his quest to conquer the information superhighway, Gates cheerfully expects to lose at least $1 billion over the next two to three years before he sees a profit. In the longer term, however, the company believes that annual revenues of about $13 billion to $15 billion will be generated on the Net by the year 2000. In the 1997 to 2000 window, Microsoft aims to capture 10 per cent of that business. Advertising spending on the Net is expected to rise from $200 million a year at the outset of 1997 to at least $3 billion by the year 2000.[65] Microsoft seems to be setting its eyes on about $1 billion of this from its online service.

Media Futures

While apparently, and resolutely, sticking to its software knitting, Microsoft also seems intent on expanding its media interests.

For a dominant software company, this is perhaps a strange and somewhat puzzling move, for, at the moment, software companies are generally valued at much higher multiples of earnings than are media companies. Why then should the $8.7 billion software monolith, which literally controls more than 85 per cent of the PCs on the planet, want to move out of the high-profit, high-margin safety zone of software sales into the more risky, hits-driven media business. Why indeed? The answer lies in how you read the tea leaves of the software industry.

Just like Murdoch is heavily overstretched financially, allegedly, some think that Gates is losing his touch. In 1995 he was wrong about the Internet, he was wrong about Java (the computer language) and he was wrong about the NC. Moreover, some analysts believe the software revenue stream to be vulnerable. Though still growing at 17 per cent per annum, the personal computer market must reach saturation at some point, and surely program upgrades and speed improvements cannot continue on an infinite expansion path. Perhaps in part this explains Gates's move into the media business. At the very least, he is seriously hedging his strategic bets.

Thus, though the company continues to assert that software for PCs is its primary business, over the past two years Microsoft has methodically placed significant amounts of capital, staff and corporate resources on varied interactive media ploys, resulting in a strategy that encompasses everything from the creation of media assets to the invention of next-generation online computing technology. With markets for word processors and spreadsheets maturing, Microsoft is expanding elsewhere. Interactive products and services offer an entrée into the wired world and an opportunity for the company to learn about the content business.

With an annual research budget of more than $2 billion, Microsoft is putting much of its efforts into ambitious 'high reach' projects. It is also spending in the region of $400 million annually on media projects. MSN's broadcasting channel development is part of Microsoft's drive towards original content-production which was illustrated by the Seattle company's $30 million joint venture with production firm DreamWorks SKG; the MSNBC news-gathering broadcasting venture with the US TV network NBC; and the launch of its electronic magazine *Slate* in 1996. The joint venture with NBC has led to MSNBC, which is both a 24-hour news service on cable

TV and an Internet TV channel (see case study in Chapter 5). In association with NBC, Microsoft will invest $440 million over five years in MSNBC. Also indicative of Microsoft's growing strategic commitment to media is the expensive new Microsoft campus, RedWest, complete with digital production and design studios that were specially built for the Interactive Media Division of 2,000 employees – a very physical manifestation of a very virtual commitment. The division is actively building a library of brand name media assets.

It has also lined up interactive distribution deals with companies ranging from national Internet service providers (UUNet) to direct broadcast satellite companies (DirecTV). In April 1997, Microsoft paid $425 million to acquire WebTV Networks, a Silicon Valley company which has developed technology to enable customers to surf the Net on their television sets without purchasing a PC. Microsoft's Internet Explorer browser, developed in the face of Netscape's competition, and Windows CE operating system for pocket computers will be incorporated in WebTV products. The acquisition is a mark of Microsoft's determination to play a leading role in the convergence of personal computing, online information services and consumer electronics.

In May 1997, Microsoft and Boeing announced a futuristic, and most would say decidedly risky, $9 billion scheme to ring the earth with 324 Internet satellites. Teledesic, the company behind the scheme, claims it will create an 'Internet in the sky' and enable anyone from Africa to Antarctica to load information sixty times faster than they can at the moment with the fastest phone modems. Full-motion video teleconferencing and all other interactive multimedia applications will be possible. Decried by its critics as 'insanely expensive, insanely risky and insanely unmanageable' or simply as insane, Teledesic is no ordinary start-up. Bill Gates and Craig McCaw (who pioneered cellular telephony with his firm McCaw Cellular, selling it to AT&T in 1994), its two founders and principal shareholders, have confounded naysayers before and, despite the formidable obstacles ahead, they may do so again, however outlandish the scheme may appear to us earth-bound mortals.

Thus, over the past few years, Microsoft has been stockpiling advanced technology assets that target, with surgical precision, each area where the creation and distribution of media are headed, from visual computing to high-speed, interactive digital video. On to the foundation of a software distribution monopoly it is grafting expertise; it is developing its own technology tools and researching deeply into interactivity, human interfaces and visual computing. Not only is it forging major media and hardware alliances, it is using its deep pockets and ubiquitous brand awareness to define a unique global presence.

Despite this spurt of growth into new media, for now at least, the PC-based media occupy a tiny niche compared with classical content, delivered by media giants like Disney, Time Warner and Viacom, and interactive media will remain a small business for Microsoft in the short term. However, if the current levels of investment in media continue or increase, the company will eventually have to acknowledge that media is one of Microsoft's strategic businesses. So, whether by circumstance or design, by the year 2000 Microsoft will be holding many pieces of the new media and creative technology jigsaw puzzle. It will also critically control the entire value chain of delivering new media – PC software, Internet access, servers and creative tools.

In 1995, the idea that a computer software 'geek' might go into media raised incredulous laughter in both industries. Yet, shortly before the close of 1996, Gates signalled that he was already there when he split Microsoft into two divisions, one handling its traditional software business and the other concentrating on the media. Now there are fears that, before 1998 is over, Gates will control the bulk of online news and entertainment on the Internet just as he controls 90 per cent of the PC software market.

NEWS CORPORATION
The Media Mogul

In 1996, Rupert Murdoch, chairman of News Corporation, became the biggest owner of television stations in the USA with the $2.5 billion purchase of the 80 per cent of the New World Communications chain of ten stations he did not already own. He also finally realised his ambition to launch Fox News, the television news channel he hopes to take around the world. Perhaps the most significant development, however, was his commitment to invest approaching $2 billion to launch digital satellite television in the

UK, the USA, Japan and India. He is now the most powerful media tycoon in history in terms of his company's global reach and the diversity of its media interests.

The start was relatively inconspicuous with no obvious portent of things to come. Rupert Murdoch started out in 1952 as the owner of two Adelaide newspapers. In the forty-five years that have elapsed since then, News Corp, founded in 1979, has grown into the world's fourth largest media group and the world's largest newspaper publisher. News Corp., 36 per cent owned by the Murdoch family, with its headquarters in Sydney, Australia, owns over 100 newspapers and magazines around the world, notably the *Sun* and *The Times* (UK), *The Australian* (Australia) and *TV Guide*, the second most popular publication in the States. In terms of satellite interests, News Corp. owns 40 per cent of British Sky Broadcasting (BSkyB), the UK satellite system, with almost 6 million subscribers. It is launching an Indian and a Japanese version of Sky (ISkyB and JSkyB respectively) in 1998 and is developing American Sky Broadcasting (ASkyB) in the States. Significantly, the company also controls StarTV, an Asian satellite TV service.

Murdoch's business interests span the globe: in the USA, Germany, Italy, South America, UK, India, China and Australia. Moreover, he has an impressive array of media assets in the States including Fox Television stations, New World Communications Corporation, the *New York Post*, the *Standard*, Twentieth Century Fox Film Corporation, HarperCollins, and smaller ventures like *TV Guide*, World League Football, Fox Interactive, and the fX channel. Meanwhile in the UK, his primary interests are the News International vehicle – which owns approximately one-third of all the national newspapers sold in Britain including the *Sun*, the *News of the World*, *The Times* and the *Sunday Times* – and also BSkyB, of which News Corp. owns 40 per cent, HarperCollins UK and News Datacom. By 1996, there were, in all, twenty-one satellite-cable channels available through multichannel package, although Sky itself runs just nine including Sky News, News Corp.'s 'own CNN' which also broadcasts in Europe, Asia and Africa.

With mogul status necessarily goes a willingness to take risks accompanied, in Murdoch's case, with a largely unfettered entrepreneurial spirit. Risk and failure are necessary precursors to success. But, as most of the key players in the content, communications or computing business know, the stakes these days are high. No wonder Andy Groves, CEO of Intel, named his latest book *Only the Paranoid Survive* and Ted Turner, Bill Gates and Rupert Murdoch have in their time been attributed the dubious accolade of demented maverick.

Maverick? Yes. Demented? Well perhaps. Certainly such competitive turmoil demands nerves of steel and a willingness to put their money where their mouth is. For example, by virtue of their large-scale investments, both the American cable companies and News Corp. are carrying immense debt burdens, and the start-up costs associated with ISkyB, ASkyB, JSkyB, Sky Latino, and Foxtel – a 50 per cent owned venture that is one of the three entrants in Australia's pay TV market – will take a heavy toll on News Corp.'s nerve and financial resources. No wonder News Corp. investors, spooked by the memories of its brush with bankruptcy, want Murdoch to rein in. Murdoch's shrewdness and business acumen are legendary, but it is not inconceivable that this time his seemingly insatiable appetite for expensive acquisitions will find him terminally wrong-footed.

However, the deals keep coming in, despite all the competitive bruising. News Corp. concluded a deal with two leading cable providers to take Fox News, the 24-hour US television news service planned by the company, into 2.5 million homes over the three years following October 1996 when the channel went live. It is planned that Fox News should have almost 15 million viewers by 1999. Further distribution channels should open up in the interim, including smaller cable groups, and News Corp.'s own satellite TV service due to launch in 1998.

Moreover, despite the repeated spats and packaged venom that pass between Ted Turner, of Turner Broadcasting Systems, and Rupert Murdoch – there is no love lost – experience shows their mutual interest takes the edge off their animosity. Like cooperating with an erstwhile competitor, mutual dependency and partnerships have become an uneasy fact of life in a converging world. Turner Broadcasting System Inc. (now part of Time Warner), Walt Disney Co. and News Corp. know that no one controls enough to shut out deals with their rivals. Competitors wind up switching between the roles of adversaries, prized customers and key partners, so no one can really afford to burn their boats irretrievably. In this world of global competition where no one – yet – holds all the ace cards, alliances, mutualities, joint ventures and serious competition all co-exist, albeit rather uneasily.

MCI Associations

As 1996 was a critical year for Rupert Murdoch, so 1995 had its moments. In May 1995, News Corp. announced a joint venture with MCI Communications. MCI, the world's second largest long-distance telecommunication company and, with Sprint, one of the primary challengers to AT&T in the States, invested $2 billion for a 13.5 per cent stake in News Corp. Both companies invested $200 million, or the equivalent in product, in the joint venture. This came hot on the heels of the acquisition of Twentieth Century Fox television stations and coincided with the early days of Fox News, the fourth US television network.

At first sight, it seemed the multimedia empire had arrived. The MCI deal, linking telecoms technology to media, aimed to create a company that could deliver information and entertainment services electronically worldwide. News Corp.'s vast library of 'software' – which includes films, television programmes and data – would travel around America on MCI's fibre optical networks, while abroad they would be transmitted on the lines run by Concert, the BT/MCI joint venture. Technologically, the deal put News Corp. directly on to one of the primary carrier systems of the superhighway. However, it seems the completion of empire might have to wait a while.

Although not as comprehensive nor as spectacular as observers had originally envisaged, this high-profile convergence of telecommunications and content was certainly the product of strategic thinking. Murdoch's link with MCI confirmed that he was hedging his bets by securing guaranteed outlets on the information superhighway for the huge bank of programmes which he had already built up, ranging from his Fox film archives (which can be continually recycled through video-on-demand technology) to US football, Premier League soccer and Rugby League. Contrast this with BT which, for the moment, is precluded by the UK government from sending entertainment down its phone lines and is, perforce, obliged to be a transmission system rather than an entertainment provider in the short term. The cable industry in the UK, understandably, sees this temporary restriction on BT as a necessary inhibition which will ensure that, after 2001, all participants in the global multimedia game play on a level field.

By October 1996 however, relations between Bert Roberts of MCI and Rupert Murdoch had begun to sour, with allegations that MCI executives were being excluded from any meaningful management role in the venture. MCI's agreed investment was for unspecified new media operations which had included ASkyB. MCI was set to own half this venture with News Corp. but the spat between the two companies forced a re-assessment of MCI's role in the new satellite TV company. The alliance was unpicked further in November of the same year when the planned takeover by BT of MCI was announced. This sent Murdoch back to the drawing board, for if the acquisition had gone ahead MCI would have been treated as a foreign company by the US regulators and thus would not have been able to hold the satellite licence. In any case, MCI now wants only 20 per cent of the satellite venture. MCI's re-assessment and scaling back of its role will unnerve investors, for the advantages of MCI's presence in the deal as a 50:50 partner included that fact that it was a 'deep-pocket' partner with substantial marketing expertise. The News Corp.-MCI partnership looks as though it may unravel. If it doesn't, however, BT is sitting with a foot in both the ASkyB digital development in the States (now thought tenuous) and BSkyB digital development in the UK.

Satellite: the Second Wave

For Murdoch, the USA is the last frontier for his global satellite empire. With News Corp.'s 40 per cent interest in BSkyB, its control of Asia's Star TV and start-ups in Latin America, its planned US service will provide the crucial link in a satellite network in all the critical global markets. His first attempt to head the pack in this highly competitive arena took the form of a $1 billion alliance with EchoStar Communications to launch a 500-channel satellite broadcasting venture.

In February 1997, News Corp. announced it would pay $500 million for a 50 per cent stake in Colorado-based EchoStar, the smallest and most entrepreneurial of America's satellite broadcasters, and would give EchoStar satellites and other assets from ASkyB, the direct-broadcast joint venture it owns with MCI Communications. The alliance was due to launch under the trading name of Sky early in 1998 with a 120-channel service, thus intensifying competition in the satellite television market in the States. They were poised to create a force that could be the biggest challenge to date to the cable giants that for three decades have dominated American television transmission and supply nearly 70 million homes, that is, two-thirds of the market.

However, barely three months after the announcements, and due in part to Murdoch's own political and business miscalculations, EchoStar filed a $5 billion lawsuit alleging that News Corp. reneged on its deal to launch the service jointly. Thus, for the moment, Murdoch is stymied, but doubtless this will not remain the case for long as there is too much at stake. News Corp. is believed to have held preliminary discussions with rival US satellite broadcast companies such as PrimeStar and DirecTV.

It won't be easy. Murdoch faces more hurdles than he has ever previously encountered. In Britain, he overwhelmed a complacent broadcasting establishment with his satellite service, quickly signing up millions of subscribers by locking up exclusive movie and sporting rights. However, the US cable industry, with 65 million subscribers and $28 billion in annual revenues, is a far more aggressive rival in local markets, as well as on Capitol Hill in Washington, and the DBS market in the USA, though fledgling, already has three strong entrants. Whichever company partners up with News Corp., its entrée into the television market will presage highly competitive combat between the *ancien régime* of cable and the aggressive and aspirational zest of the new satellite entrants.

This battle will be watched across the world for three reasons. First, developments in the USA will affect the value and cachet of Sky as a television brand. News Corp. is spreading into Asia with ISkyB in India and JSkyB in Japan as part of its push to establish the global satellite television brand. Second, the arrival of DBS and wireless transmission, with its data transmission (direct-to-home satellite broadcasting) compression will provoke serious headaches among providers of fixed-wire service that once believed their monopoly infrastructures were assets, not potential liabilities. Third, because a similar war is being fought out in Britain as BSkyB, now valued at £10 billion, takes on a more immature cable sector and one that has disappointed investors.

Meanwhile in Japan, JSkyB, the digital satellite broadcasting company established by News Corp. and Softbank, the Japanese computer software distributor and publishers, confirmed in May 1997 that Sony and Fuji TV were to join as equal partners in the venture which plans to offer 150 channels to viewers in Japan as from spring 1998. The joint venture is an important part of Murdoch's plans to take multichannel digital television systems to some of the world's developed markets in 1998 with planned launches in the USA, the UK and India to add to his digital operations in Latin America and Asia.

News Corp., through its part ownership of BSkyB, has also been doing deals as though there is no tomorrow. In the UK, satellite, cable and terrestrial digital broadcasting is due to launch in 1998, with satellite due for introduction in the spring. Throughout 1996 many commentators feared that Murdoch would drive a Trojan Horse through the digital firmament by controlling the so-called gateway to digital broadcasting – the set-top box. Given his erstwhile intention to issue a proprietary set-top box and launch this system ahead of terrestrial, if not also of cable, the fear was that he would steal a triumphant march on the fledgling digitisation of traditional British broadcasting. However, in a brilliantly pragmatic move, Murdoch at once defused the aggro, confounded his critics and presented an apparently amicable solution to a mounting impasse. As rabbits go, this was a pretty spectacular one to pull out of the hat.

In a maverick move, the terrestrial broadcasters, Granada and Carlton, joined equal forces with BSkyB to form British Digital Broadcasting (BDB) in a bid to scoop the remaining terrestrial multiplexes. Significantly, also, the BBC agreed to provide four of its pay-TV channels, developed through its BBC Worldwide venture with Flextech, to the BDB consortium. Here we had a circle of broadcasters – whether vicious or virtuous – which for the first time broke down the barriers between terrestrial and satellite, commercial and public service. However, BSkyB was subsequently forced by the industry regulator, the Independent Television Commission, to drop its equity share in the venture though it will be a primary programme supplier.

The key question in all of these developments is whether such a loaded multichannel environment is financially viable. Despite the forty-odd cable and satellite channels launched in the UK since the mid 1980s, it is still the case that over 75 per cent of UK homes choose not to connect to either cable or satellite.

While pay-per-view sport and near video-on-demand movies may very well remain the drivers of subscription television, can each micro-channel of the hundreds projected really draw sufficient audience numbers to make the figures stack up? Clearly BSkyB believes that they will. What is certain though is that the three-channel television environment of the early 1980s and indeed the 40-odd-channel environment of 1997 will soon become a curious arcane feature of the last twenty years of the twentieth century. While the emergence of digital transmission will cause only a gradual erosion of viewing share for the existing channels, the phenomenal growth in subscription income – particularly through digital TV – will change the financing model which underpins the industry in the UK and indeed the entire balance of power within the industry itself.

The Net Connection

After a decade of preparing the ground, Murdoch made a significant breakthrough into the biggest market in the world. It was not in the States and it was not satellite television – it was in China and it was the Internet.

It was an important development. What may at first have seemed an unspectacular coup in fact carried the possibility of entrée into the Chinese market, and access to a fifth of the world's population. In 1995, Murdoch and the *People's Daily* agreed to a $5.4 billion 20-year joint venture to cooperate in disseminating information technology. About $2.5 billion has been invested in ChinaByte, a Chinese language Web site providing computer industry information, most of it from News Corp., which hopes its investment will be recouped from advertising. ChinaByte has been developed by the News Corp.-*People's Daily* joint venture in partnership with Ziff-Davis, a New York-based publisher of computer magazines and acquired by Softbank, Japan's largest distributor of computer software.

Murdoch had been seeking a foothold since the early 1980s but had previously been frustrated by Chinese suspicions of his intentions. These were exacerbated in 1993 when Murdoch said satellite television posed an 'unambiguous threat to totalitarian regimes everywhere'. This did not please Beijing and Murdoch's efforts to extend the reach of Star TV network in China were thwarted. He did, however, in part at least, redeem himself in May

1997 in a keynote speech about mass communications, saying, 'The Chinese leadership has proved the sceptics, including myself, wrong by not shunning the new information technologies but actively encouraging their use.'

The ChinaByte development is both a calling card for Murdoch's plans to become a major TV force in China and also his recognition, along with Bill Gates in 1996, that the Internet has become the most powerful force of the information revolution. As Murdoch himself said in December 1996, 'The Internet is bearing down on us like a fast train and we have to decide do we get on it or do we jump off the track.'[66] It looks as if Murdoch has clambered on board, although rather cautiously. He was, though, one of the first to seek an investment back in 1993 – a positively antediluvian era by Internet standards – with Delphi Internet. As it transpired Delphi, an Internet access service, eventually pressed the self-destruct button and died, a witness to the fact that both Bill Gates and Rupert Murdoch have found the Internet a rather slithery eel, both having made various attempts to approach it from different angles.

Apart from ChinaByte, News Corp. has two Internet projects on the cards. One is the new Web site called the *TV Guide* Entertainment Network which has the contents of the News Corp. weekly magazine, plus original articles on movies, television, pop music and sports. It plans to capitalise on the magazine's popularity and piggy-back on the brand recognition factor. The second is the LineOne Internet service launched in the UK by News Corp. and its ally BT in early 1997.

Moreover, Murdoch's global digital TV service will offer Internet-related services as well. In the UK, BSkyB, his satellite television venture, plans to offer fast access to the Internet through conventional television sets when it launches its digital satellite television service. Doubtless the interactive services will be phased in in a commercially astute fashion. Here, though, digital satellite is threatened by digital cable which is technically superior for two-way broadband communications. However, as Murdoch has proven in the past with his technically inferior satellite television systems, it is not sophistication that necessarily wins out in the commercial battle stakes, but business acumen. And Murdoch has this – in buckets.

BRITISH TELECOMMUNICATIONS
Going Private

British Telecommunications (BT) was a classic utility in every sense of the word before its privatisation in 1984. Privatisation, and a significantly keener competitive market, was instigated, in part, due to rapidly advancing technology. Telecommunications were no longer a national monopoly, requiring huge fixed investments in copper cable and mechanical switches. Competitors wielded fibre optic cables, capable of carrying 1.2 million simultaneous calls, and compact computers and sophisticated microprocessors for switching. As these appeared on the scene and began to invade the communications market, politicians came to realise that efficient communications was an important engine for economic growth.

However, despite privatisation in 1984, and despite challenges from Mercury Communications, the UK market remained an effective BT monopoly throughout the 1980s. In an effort to introduce more competition, the government dismantled the BT-Mercury duopoly in 1991 and allowed cable companies to use their networks for telephony as well as TV services, whilst precluding BT from entering the field of entertainment broadcasting. Despite this, according to Oftel, the telecoms industry regulator, BT still controlled about 80 per cent of the overall telecoms market in 1996, having less than two-thirds of the market for international calls, but 90 per cent of the market for local calls.

At the end of 1996, it was announced that Britain was to make its largest single move towards opening up its international telecoms market to competition. As in the USA, technological advances acted as a catalyst for this second wave of deregulation. Licences were on offer for companies, including AT&T and Global One, seeking to compete with BT and Mercury Communications in offering a full range of telecoms services between the UK and the rest of the world. In the past, companies had only been able to operate by leasing lines from one of the two British companies, but now they will be in a position to build and operate their own infrastructure. The UK is the first country to open its international market fully to competition in this way.

The biggest challenge to BT's dominance of the UK telecoms market came in April 1997 when Cable & Wireless Communications (CWC) was listed on the London and New York stock markets. CWC was formed in October 1996 from the merger of Mercury Communications (Cable & Wireless's UK telecoms business) and the three leading cable companies – UK cable groups with North American parents – Bell Cablemedia, Nynex CableComms Group and Videotron Holdings. Through this major realignment, CWC acquired, at a stroke, a 10 per cent share of the £21 billion fixed and mobile UK telephone market, against BT's 67 per cent. The merger also created by far the largest of the cable companies. As CWC knows, critical mass and the economies of scale it brings are vital for a successful telecoms company.

The dominance of BT in the telecoms market and BSkyB in the non-terrestrial television market present CWC with formidable competition, but this is not something its chief executive, Dick Brown, is likely to shy away from. Analysts project that the new company, if marketed properly, could take 25 per cent of BT's market over the next five years. Moreover, CWC's ambitions are not merely UK-wide, but global. Prior to the four-way merger in the UK, Dick Brown pulled off a successful negotiation with the German conglomerate RWE, snatching partnership from under the noses of BT and Viag. CWC is also likely to be the vehicle for closer ties with French and German telecom companies: Deutsche Telekom and France Telecom are understood to be interested in joining CWC after its flotation, replacing the North American cable groups. This would knit the company into one of the most powerful telecoms groupings. The next deal is likely to be in America, where a tie-up with a partner such as Nynex could unlock the value of CWC's American business – and then there is the challenge of sustaining a lucrative stake in Hong Kong and staving off Chinese predatory instincts. Clearly this is not a business for the faint-hearted.

Ironically, BT and Cable & Wireless were themselves in negotiations to merge in 1996. The Cable & Wireless deal would have offered BT a lucrative slice of the Asian markets via C&W's stake in Hongkong Telecom, the main carrot for BT, and thus stretched BT's global reach eastwards. It would have secured a bridgehead into Hong Kong and a chance to break into the Chinese market, but the deal would have involved a myriad government hurdles, the divesting of Mercury Communications, and a cost of up to £10 billion to buy out minority interest in Hongkong Telecom and pay a special dividend to C&W shareholders. The luckless deal faced a barrage of regulatory, political and business obstacles and eventually collapsed under the weight of its own difficulties.

The MCI Connection

The expectation that market deregulation and liberalisation will lead to increased competition and lower profit margins has lead BT to expand abroad. Most observers would regard this strategy as sound, though some would question the wisdom of the chosen route. The BT–MCI partnership started in 1993 when BT paid $4.2 billion for a 20 per cent stake in MCI, America's second largest long-distance telephone company, and launched a joint venture called Concert. By 1995, the original Concert – the proposed BT–MCI merged company was also to be known as Concert – was focused on providing worldwide telephone and electronic services to the 5,000 or so large international companies that require reliable, bespoke communications worldwide. Then, in 1996, the US Telecommunications Act set in train the deregulation of the US local telecom monopolies. The hitherto separate cable-TV companies, baby Bells and long-distance telephone carriers were released from their territorially defined boundaries and allowed to pitch in each other's territory. This offered a lucrative market opportunity for a company which could offer a single, unified telecoms service across local, national and international boundaries. Enter MCI as a competitor.

However, in order to compete effectively MCI required financial muscle and, ideally, an internationally-based partner. It needed to look no further than BT and the proposed merger between the two companies was announced in November 1996. The scale of the merger took the financial world by surprise. At £10.5 billion this was the largest proposed takeover in UK corporate history, just eclipsing the £10 billion merger of SmithKline Beckman and Beecham Group, and Glaxo's £8.9 billion takeover of Wellcome. The original proposed deal at £13 billion before it was negotiated down would have ranked it as the second biggest deal in the USA, behind Kohlberg Kravis Roberts' $24 billion leveraged buyout of RJR Nabisco. Clearly this is a serious business.

With $43 billion in combined revenues, the merged company would have had a 20 per cent share of the US long-distance market, a 90 per cent share of the domestic UK local and long-distance market, and network facilities in thirty countries. Though smaller in monetary value than AT&T, the global reach of the company would have made it the world's largest international telecoms company, eclipsing both AT&T and NTT of Japan: that is, if the deal had not been unravelled by the US group WorldCom which placed a surprise $37 billion counterbid for MCI in November 1997.

While the acquisition of MCI would have virtually doubled BT's size at a stroke and made it one of the world's largest telecoms players, the American market is no picnic. MCI's pre-tax profit margins are typically less than half that of BT's, and in 1996 MCI earned a return of 6 per cent against BT's 21 per cent. To make matters worse, MCI announced in July 1997 that breaking into the US local telephone market would cost it an extra $1.8 billion over the following two years – hardly music to the ears of BT shareholders.[67] MCI's profit margins are likely to fall before they rise. Moreover, more competitors are entering the international calls market, MCI's core business, and the company has found no easy route into the higher-margin local market.

As MCI knows, the complexity and challenge of the US phone market cannot be underestimated. In 1995, the Telecommunications Act ostensibly opened up the long-distance and local markets to all-comers. The result was a flurry of deals among the local phone companies, culminating in Bell Atlantic's merger with Nynex. The combined 'baby Bell' has seamless coverage down most of the eastern seaboard, and is now allowed to route long-distance calls, at no cost, along its network.

However, backed by WorldCom's financial muscle, MCI says it will be a stronger competitor not just for AT&T, but for each of the local Bells. It is the combination of WorldCom's entrepreneurial spirit and MCI's well-known eagerness for a fight that has shaken the rest of the US telecommunications industry and, when the merger was announced, prompted a search on Wall Street for another wave of giant telecommunication mergers, for financial strength is a *sine qua non* for competitive edge in a marketplace. It is also a matter of marketing, as well as capital spending, at a time when profit margins will be under pressure from increased competition. To demonstrate the point, CW&C in the UK has, for example, earmarked £50 million on an advertising campaign due to start in the late autumn of 1997. Though clearly a substantial amount of money, this is but a quarter of BT's annual advertising budget.

Meanwhile, in the UK, deregulation in BT's backyard opens its home base market up to competition from America, Continental Europe and Asia. BT retains command of the business and residential market in the UK, but its lead is being steadily eroded by AT&T's aggressive offers to the business community, and by the cable companies efforts in the residential market. Turning the deregulated market on both sides of the Atlantic in its favour must be the first priority for BT post the WorldCom announcement. If BT, possibly with another partner, could achieve a solid market position in the States and maintain its dominance in the UK, there would seem to be little stopping it from sweeping weaker and more parochial European brethren before it.

It's Good to Deal

The glare of publicity which surrounded BT's announcement of its merger with MCI obscured the quiet determination with which the UK operator had been pursuing its international strategy. During the 1993 to 1997 period, BT signed an astonishing thirty-eight international deals, gradually sewing up different patches of the marketplace. Nevertheless, BT and MCI between them have a mere 6 per cent of the $670 billion global telecoms market and more than 80 per cent of that market is still closed to competition, though a wave of liberalisation is opening up a host of opportunities. EU markets, for example, collectively valued at about $192 billion a year, are due to open to full competition in January 1998.

After announcing the proposed MCI merger, BT began pursuing international partnerships more aggressively through its Concert alliance. Concert is seeking to create an international telecoms infrastructure which will connect to regional carriers in local markets in a bid to outmanoeuvre its competitors. In this elite league there are three key global alliances, namely Cable & Wireless's Global One partnership, a grouping of Sprint of the USA with Deutsche Telekom and France Telecom; WorldPartners, which comprises AT&T, Singapore Telecom, Indosat and others; and Concert itself. By the end of the century, the world's telecoms needs will be controlled by three or four major groupings, alliances formed through mergers, equity swaps and contractual agreements and BT is positioning itself at the forefront of the shakeout in the industry.

Recent deals in Continental Europe and India illustrate BT's global expansion policy. In January 1997 it announced the acquisition of a 22.5 per cent stake in Bharti Cellular (BCL), the largest mobile operator in India, and state-owned Indian operator VSNL (Videsh Sanchar Nigam) is intent on signing a partnership agreement with BT. This partnership is said to be investing up to $550 million to build a high-capacity hub which will transport voice, data, and Internet traffic between India, Sri Lanka, Bangladesh and Pakistan. Analysts expect the planned venture to yield more than $1 billion in revenues within ten years. The deal will give BT a firm foothold in the fast growing Indian telecoms market, and provide further important links in its expansion programme.

Meanwhile, the ink was hardly dry on the BT-MCI merger announcement papers when the new company launched into negotiations with companies in Spain and Portugal to forge links which open up lines to the critical Latin American market. In addition to a deal with Portugal Telecom, which joins the Concert alliance as a strategic partner, BT and MCI also concluded a deal with Spain's Telefonica. This was a blow to America's AT&T which was tipped as Telefonica's favoured international partner.

The Portuguese and Spanish deals have even greater significance, for Portugal Telecom offers Concert a clear path into Brazil through its link with Telebras, the state-owned operator that is being privatised. Likewise, Telefonica, which is one of the world's top ten telecoms groups, and the biggest player in the Spanish speaking world, is part of a consortium that controls CRT, an important Brazilian operator. Moreover, it has controlling stakes or equity investments in Chile, Peru, Argentina, Brazil and Puerto Rico.

Thus, through its two deals with Portugal Telecom and Telefonica of Spain, Concert has secured a firm route into one of the world's most important telecoms markets that is expected to see phenomenal growth over the next few years: Latin America. It is a market estimated to be worth between $35 billion and $40 billion now in terms of telecoms revenue, but is expected to boom to between $60 billion and $65 billion by the year 2000.[68] However, this prize will not be won easily. A considerable amount of work will need to be done by Concert over the coming years, by way of infrastructure investment, marketing and developing new territories, to ensure it exploits its new-found geographic reach to the full.

The Telefonica deal completes the series of alliances planned by BT in Europe that includes France (with Cegetel), Germany (with Viag Interkom), the Netherlands (with Telfort) and Italy (with Albacom), and leaves the Asian Pacific Rim as the important remaining strategic gap in its efforts with MCI to span the globe. The sights of Concert strategists are thus already set on this remaining and internationally critical uncharted territory, but transforming a transatlantic tryst into a global *ménage à trois* will not be easy. Together with India, as Global One, WorldPartners and Concert know, China and Japan are the key remaining markets to grasp in any global strategy, but these are difficult territories to penetrate. Although there are other possible partners, NTT, the Japanese giant, is the prize that Concert, Global One and WorldPartners would dearly love to land.

Digital Connections

Over the last three years, BT has begun to explore the development of products and services in the digital domain and to nudge itself towards a multimedia future, for it is not so fanciful, as it once was, to contemplate that the Internet is growing so strongly and becoming so versatile that it may one day become the main medium for television and (voice) phone calls as well as computer-led communications. Here, as in voice telephony, BT finds itself in competition with cable-based communication networks.

In 1995, BT launched an interactive television trial in East Anglia in the UK, based on ADSL technology (asymmetric digital subscriber line), to provide enhanced broadband connections. The trial was designed to establish the potential demand for interactive multimedia services – including electronic shopping, home banking, video-on-demand, and interactive games – delivered over high bandwidth, in this case a two megabytes per second signal. This trial paralleled similar trials in the States including Time Warner's Full Service Network and Viacom's California trial.

These trials were hampered by a combination of technical snags, rising costs, regulatory hurdles and an unenthusiastic customer base. Inevitably, perhaps, a fading sense of urgency entered the proceedings with the realisation that commercial roll-out, and thus commercial returns, would take longer than anticipated. Moreover, interactive television has been somewhat overshadowed by the new technical and economic model that digital television assumes. Additionally, the cost of developing such a sophisticated network is now seen as effectively non-viable in relation to anticipated commercial returns. Thus BT has estimated the cost of upgrading its entire UK network to consist of high-capacity fibre cables to be in the region of £15 billion. However, it has indicated its intention to connect all schools, libraries and hospitals to a fibre-optic 'superhighway' and continues to apply pressure for the early retraction of legislation currently preventing it from broadcasting entertainment services on its network.

In September 1995, BT launched CampusWorld, an online Internet service dedicated to education, and in 1996 introduced BT Internet, an Internet access service aimed at residential and small business customers. BT also announced the planned launch of Touchpoint, a networked interactive multimedia kiosk service, and Wireplay, a nationwide dedicated computer games network. Meanwhile, MCI formed a broad alliance with Microsoft in early 1996 and extended that partnership in the spring of 1997 to provide combined software and communications capacity to US companies setting up intranets. In August 1996, BT began to encourage individual subscribers to its Internet access service to use Microsoft's Explorer software rather than Netscape's Navigator browser. In the USA, AT&T, BT's main international rival and MCI's main domestic rival, has also promoted Microsoft in its rapidly expanding Internet access service, while Global One, the third largest international alliance, appears increasingly inclined towards Netscape. Experimentation and innovation in the area of networked multimedia was extended further in 1997 with the launch, jointly with News International in the UK of the Internet access service, LineOne, and with its involvement in the British Interactive Broadcasting (BIB) consortium.

BIB is a consortium composed of BT, BSkyB, the Midland Bank and Matsushita, the Japanese electronics company, and has been formed to sell subsidised digital TV decoder boxes. The four partners are investing £265 million over five years, with BT and BSkyB each holding a 32.5 per cent interest in the new venture. Each of the partners obviously has a vested interest in the digital transmission of hundreds of channels and interactive services, with BT hoping to gain from providing a return path – and thus increased line usage – for the interactive services delivered via digital transmission, though here again BT will be challenged by the cable companies and their launch of digital cable services. Many analysts agree that cable is the only system that has the capacity to provide true interactivity, but, as Rupert Murdoch knows only too well, it is not necessarily the superior technology which wins in the marketplace but, rather, a sufficient technology with superior marketing backed by deep financial resources, shrewd business judgement and corporate patience.

BT was also, in a more umbilical way, linked to News Corp. through MCI's 20 per cent ownership share of Rupert Murdoch's company. On the face of things, the BT-MCI link would have reinforced the alliance between BT and BSkyB, although the impact of the link should perhaps not be exaggerated for BT's economic interest in BSkyB would still have been fairly small. Indeed BT and MCI de-emphasised their links with News Corp. when they announced their deal. Murdoch, who now sits on MCI's board, will not be a director of Concert, and MCI is planning to cut its participation in ASkyB, a US satellite joint venture with Murdoch.

It is still true, though, that the fortunes of News Corp., Microsoft and Concert, the BT/MCI partnership, are intertwined and that their future prospects are each dependent on the development of digital technology and networked communications as they each know from different digital perspectives, this technology is the driving force behind the digital revolution and the transition to post-modern society.

Chapter 5

Micro Reforms

VIRGIN TERRAIN

This chapter gives an insight into the business models adopted by a range of digital pioneers. The first three companies – MSNBC, the *Wall Street Journal* and the Wells Fargo Bank – have a presence in both the physical and the virtual world. The *Wall Street Journal* and the Wells Fargo Bank have long established histories: the Wells Fargo Bank having been founded in 1852 and the *Wall Street Journal* in 1889. By contrast, Microsoft and NBC (National Broadcast Corporation), the two parent companies of MSNBC, are relatively new companies, though positively historic in new technology years, being founded in 1975 and 1926 respectively.

All four companies have established reputations and brands instantly recognisable in the States, and familiar to business executives and professionals around the world. They illustrate how established, even conventional, companies can migrate aspects of their business to the virtual world and seek to combine the advantages of the marketplace with those of the market-space. MSNBC and the Wells Fargo Bank have been selected as examples of broadcasting and banking companies which have moved some of their business functions into cyberspace and thus have begun the process of morphing their business (see Chapter 3). Meanwhile the *Wall Street Journal* provides an illuminating example of how a publisher or broadcaster of news can combine an established print publishing business with an innovative electronic broadcasting business in a financial context where immediacy of delivery is a critical aspect of brand value.

Ten other companies are profiled in this chapter: Electronic Share

Information, Firefly, the Internet Bookshop, Peapod, PhotoDisc, Salon, Security First Network Bank, SSEYO, Travelocity and Virtual Vineyards. Each of them exists only virtually, in the sense that they trade exclusively on the Internet. In six out of these ten virtual companies – Digital Photoshop, Electronic Share Information, Firefly, Salon, Security First Network Bank and SSEYO – the actual product or service traded is also digitally composed and digitally delivered. As befits the recent upsurge of the Internet, these companies are no more than 36 months old, and are thus relatively small and highly entrepreneurial. Each illustrates how its business presence is virtually defined, how the process of commerce is virtually conducted and how it brings its products or services to the marketspace.

Like many start-ups on the Net, they tend to be media- or information-related, thus deriving their value as a product from their timeliness: here instant global presence is a critical business advantage. Moreover, in most cases the product concerned is highly amenable to digital transmission. In other cases, like that of Virtual Vineyards, a niche product is offered and made highly accessible. Clearly here there needs to be a strong correlation between the characteristics of these niche customers and the demographics of Internet users. Virtual Vineyards' speciality, artisan-originating wines, have a particular attraction to upmarket customers, while the readership profile for Salon, an electronic magazine or e-zine, is highly educated and equally up-market. Both correlate closely with the demographics of Internet users and a technology-orientated early adopter market.

Another characteristic of commercial sites on the Internet is the way in which they tend to combine product expertise with technology expertise or software engineering skills – that is, they blend art and science or creativity and technology. Thus photographers, journalists, writers and musicians – in respect, for example, of PhotoDisc, Salon, the Internet Bookshop and SSEYO – originate, commission or design the products being traded and their representation on the Net. Meanwhile technicians are essential for the design and development of the hardware and software which, in combination, make this channel to market operational. Thus Salon, for instance, employs both a commissioning editor and a director of technology/Webmaster. The key creative talent providing PhotoDisc with its trading product is the 100-plus professional photographers who supply the company's bank of digital images. Central to securing that product are the company's team of editors who vet and select the photographic images which constitute the company's key assets. In terms of bringing its products to market, or facilitating the trading process, PhotoDisc's Web team includes a 'Webmaster', programmers, producers, graphic designers, marketing planners, customer service staff, technical support staff, database experts, forum managers and systems administrators.

Virtual Vineyards describes its management team as combining wine and speciality food retailing expertise with the engineering skills needed to develop and maintain a commercial site on the Web. Its key personnel are the General Manager and Co-Founder, the President and Co-Founder, the Chairman, the Food Shop Proprietor and the Master Sommelier. Indicative of the blend of expertise required in this virtual retail environment, one of the two co-founders has been a professional wine buyer for more than fifteen years and is a master sommelier with membership of the British Court of Master Sommeliers. Meanwhile, the other co-founder has spent more than twenty-one years in system design, real-time operating systems, software development, engineering management and marketing with a corporate background in ELXSI, Hewlett-Packard and Silicon Graphics.

As befits pioneers and innovators many have won awards. Salon, for example, has won accolades as Advertising Age's Online Magazine of the Year and was named the Best Web Site of 1996 by *Time* magazine. SSEYO was awarded the PC Format Gold Award for its Koan X Platinum product. The Internet Bookshop has been widely acclaimed as a pioneer in the field while ESI won the 1996 Superhighway Award, co-sponsored by BT and the *Sunday Times*. It was also voted the best personal investment Web site in March 1997 by the *Wall Street Journal* Europe. Meanwhile PhotoDisc has pioneered secure online purchasing of print-ready images using RSA encryption, on-the-fly credit card authorisation in real time, and Shockwave animated objects (embedded animation sequences). *PC Week* recognised PhotoDisc by awarding it its Top 10 Internet Commercial Sites award and the Washington Software and Digital Media Alliance named it 'Best Business Product of the Year'.

However, these accolades have not necessarily been easily won. Much courage, soul-searching, persistence and moments of grief

have been experienced by these pioneers: like any fledgling enterprise, their business has demanded adequate financial resources,
exceptionally talented people, a clear and inspiring vision of the
future and an unshakable belief that the business rabbit can be
pulled out of the entrepreneurial hat. They have lived by the
maxim that only those who tackle the impossible will achieve the
unattainable.

As in the Malaysian Super Corridor (see Regional Hot Spots
section in Chapter 7) where they are literally creating a cyberzone
out of a jungle, the digital pioneers are cutting a virtual path through
a cyber jungle. Many obstacles have strewn their way and numerous
hurdles remain. In a presentation at the US conference Seybold 97,
Tom Hughes, president of PhotoDisc warned digital entrepreneurs
of the dangers of digital hype and the pitfalls of being offered 'silicon
snake oil', as if in the Wild West of nineteenth-century America.[69]
Some snake oil is not even advertised as such, for even the most
reputable hardware or software company can inadvertently hype a
product beyond its operational performance. Such misadventure is
intrinsic to an innovatory environment.

Tom Hughes identified five pitfalls that can snare a virtual
entrepreneur: first, the technology is often several months or a
year away from actually being implemented. For example, in
the autumn of 1997, the tools for commerce, secure credit card
transactions, broadcast e-mail and data analysis still aren't entirely
bug-free and as robust as is needed for industrial strength. The
SET standard (secure electronic transaction protocol) has helped
but is not in widespread use yet. According to Hughes, things are
improving all the time but '. . . many new entrants are not ready
for prime time.' Second, cost estimates are a moving target. Hughes
notes, 'The hardware, software, human resources and additional
staff needed to get a site up and running are hard to get your
arms around.' According to a recent report from IDC, the average
cost of a world-class commercial site – including hardware, custom
and off-the-shelf software, and development fees – is around $1
million. Forrester Research claims that it costs between $300,000
and $3 million to build a commercial site. Third, it seems that few
off-the-shelf tools really work. Customised software is required for
secure credit card transactions, data gathering and monitoring, and
shopping carts. Fourth, the peculiarities of various browsers and
multiple versions means that often the site-builder is swamped with

options and requires complex technical support, and fifth, there is the issue of security. In the short term at least it will be important to provide alternative means of payment other than a purely electronic transaction.

Despite these potential snares, much progress has been made in cutting a path through the digital jungle. Much like explorers of the physical environment, explorers of the virtual world must be courageous, pragmatic and adaptive and, moreover, be willing to weather uncertainty and discontinuity. A trek into the heart of virtual terrain is not for the faint-hearted, nor are the rewards necessarily instant, but new landscapes deliver new perspectives and new perspectives offer new prospects. Many will go prospecting and a few will be truly triumphant.

DUAL PRESENCE

MSNBC

In July 1996, Microsoft, the computer software company, and NBC (National Broadcasting Corporation), the American network television station, launched their joint venture, MSNBC, a 24-hour news service distributed on cable television and the Internet (http://www.msnbc.com). NBC is running the cable side from Secaucus in New Jersey on the east coast of the USA, and Microsoft is running the Internet part from Redmond, Seattle, Washington, on the west coast. The news service has also been developed further using the global reach of the Internet. Thus, for example, Internet MSNBC announced plans to launch ZDF-MSNBC in August 1997, a German-language version of its online service in collaboration with ZDF, Germany's leading television-news network.

MSNBC aims to become one brand with two operations – a 'conventional' cable television arm in Fort Lee and a multimedia, interactive Internet arm in Redmond. MSNBC Cable is funded from carriage fees from cable operators and advertising revenue, while Internet MSNBC derives its revenue from MSN subscriber fees (even though MSNBC is on the 'free' side of the MSN subscription wall) and from advertising. The synergy of MSNBC Cable is designed to drive demand for Internet MSNBC and vice versa.

Programmes are developed simultaneously for cable and the Internet, with some original material created for the Web. The goal is cross-pollination and an explicit marriage of Internet, television and computer software. MSNBC journalists are constantly searching for ways to make television and the Internet compatible, and to create material for the Internet complementary to what's on NBC, CNBC (NBC's cable station) and cable MSNBC. The Internet MSNBC newsroom in Redmond and the MSNBC Cable newsroom in Secaucus are in constant touch, both in a series of meetings throughout the day and via intercom day and night; and, for example, documentary reporting will appear on Cable and the Internet from MSNBC's Cable programme *Time and Again* or investigative pieces tied to NBC's *Dateline*. Thus convergence goes beyond just featuring anchor biography and programme schedules on the Internet service and into shared news content and complementary programming.

While striving to operate in sync with its cable counterpart, Internet MSNBC is experimenting with new ways to break news and relay stories, to integrate different media, and to deploy software to enhance interactivity, and thus with different ways of digesting the news. It uses material both from NBC news and from wire services, and generates its own original journalism, both from its own staff of sixty journalists, and from the network's television correspondents, who sometimes file audio reports just for the site.

Internet MSNBC also develops Web features that complement NBC's TV news stories. For example, coinciding with topicality on the cable channel, it has offered special sections on the NFL draft, on the civil war in Zaire and provided a guide to all the players in the campaign-finance scandals. In terms of local topicality, to complement an NBC TV report on dangerous roads, the Web site put up a feature where readers could check out lethal roads in their own areas.

Traditional, established journalists have been attracted to MSNBC from such news organisations as the *Wall Street Journal*, US News and World Report, ABC News, the Associated Press, CBS News and the *Los Angeles Times*. For example, Sheila Kaplan, a former investigative producer for ABC, now produces special reports for MSNBC; former CBS producer, Michael Silberman, is MSNBC's executive editor; and, Merrill Brown, editor-in-chief of Internet MSNBC, combines business, editorial and marketing expertise with a background in newspaper and magazine publishing and cable network management.

On the Web, MSNBC can either be accessed directly or accessed via the MSN (Microsoft Network) site (http://www.msn.com). If the latter route, then clicking on the 'On Stage' MSN option, gives you a series of options including MSNBC which jostles with Entertainment Tonight, Mungo Park, Slate, Star Trek: Continuum, Special Events, Hot Offers, Car Talk, and, Project: Watchfire.

Internet MSNBC provides access to personalisation and delivery technology. These include: Personal Front Page, which delivers news from personally selected topics, top headlines, weather, individual stock quotes and sports scores; Personal Delivery, which sends subscribers their own personal front page via e-mail every day; Personal News Offline, which downloads personalised news for offline reading; and, Personal News Alert, which provides instant notification of breaking news.

The options at the MSNBC site indicate the variety of interactive ways in which the 'channel' aims to 'deliver' news. The options are: Top Stories, Breaking News, On Air, Four Day Forecast, Customise Your News, Local News, Market Updates, Latest Scores, and Interact. The cover page has the day's headlines, updated every three hours, with occasional bulletins cross-promoting its sister channel, that is, encouraging viewers to tune in to CNBC or MSNBC cable.

Wells Fargo Bank

Wells Fargo Bank is the primary subsidiary of Wells Fargo & Co. Founded in 1852, Wells Fargo operates one of the largest consumer banking businesses in the USA, serving as banker to more than 10 million households in the ten western states. The company also provides a full range of banking services to small business, commercial agribusiness and real estate customers: in addition, it is one of the nation's leading managers and administrators of mutual fund and trust assets.

Wells Fargo Bank launched its online financial services in 1989, and Internet banking in May 1995 (http://www.wellsfargo.com). This move was part of the bank's aim to develop a comprehensive, integrated retail delivery strategy for the future. Online banking is the next logical step in the Bank's strategy for delivering 'anytime, anywhere' banking to its retail customers, thus providing them with the convenience of banking at their supermarket, via the ATM, by telephone, electronically from home or via their traditional local branch.

As of May 1997, the Internet customer base was approximately 180,000. At February 1997, there were an average of 12,000 Internet banking sessions per day and approximately 450,000 hits per week at the Internet banking site. The other online banking channels to online services, apart from the Internet, are Intuit's Quicken, Microsoft Money, America Online and Prodigy. In total 300,000 customers access Wells Fargo financial services online. Dudley Nigg, executive vice president and head of Online Financial Services for Wells Fargo Bank, expects two million – one sixth of its total current customer base – by the year 2000 or 2001. He sees the Internet as a really powerful tool for moving customers from relatively high-cost channels, and particularly from traditional branch banking.

Services and products available online include balance assessment; transaction history information; money transfer between accounts; forwarding money/bill payment to anyone, anywhere in the States; and, purchasing travellers cheques, foreign currency, and cashiers cheques. Specialist Internet services include downloading banking data into personal finance software, requesting copies of past account statements and locating the nearest Wells Fargo ATM or branch.

In 1989/90 Wells Fargo introduced its first online banking service via Prodigy and the bank's proprietary direct dial software. In December 1994, the bank created a marketing and corporate image Web site, following in early 1995 with an Internet customer survey which led, in May 1995, to Wells Fargo offering customers Internet access to peruse their account balances and transaction history.

Dudley Nigg attributes the fast growth in Wells Fargo's Internet accounts to several factors. The first is the bank's geographical location. Physically, the bank has its headquarters in San Francisco on the West Coast where there is a very high proportion of technically sophisticated early adopters. A second factor is that the bank's move online occurred just when the medium's popularity was mushrooming.

The third factor is the bank's philosophy which is to see online banking as a natural extension of its basic strategy to move customers to the most convenient and lowest cost channel. Wells

Fargo's aggressive development of supermarket branches, automated machines and telephone support services are all part of that continuum, and the Internet represents, it seems, the ultimate in convenience and low cost. The intention of Internet developments is to provide flexibility and convenience for the customer whilst lowering fixed costs for the banks. Moreover, the demographic profile of Wells Fargo's Internet customers – an average age of 35, average household income of $60,000 and average education of an undergraduate college degree or higher – makes this market segment very central to Wells Fargo's business.

Analysts say the San Francisco-based bank has been innovative in re-designing its California branch network to offer different levels of service according to customer needs, from banking centres with ATMs through to full-service branches located in supermarkets. Wells Fargo now has a presence in ten or so supermarket chains in the western states including Safeway, Raley's Tom Thumb, and Albertsons. Now, according to the Bank, their customers who never use a Wells Fargo branch (25 per cent) out-number branch-only customers (20 per cent).

Wells Fargo has decided not to join the Integrion consortium composed of IBM and sixteen banks based on a closed system (see Chapter 3), but rather to join with a few technology partners and concentrate on non-proprietary software, and thus open Internet access. The Bank has committed to the Internet as its primary online delivery platform, Nigg says.

Besides its heavy push into Web-based retail banking, Wells Fargo has been equally aggressive on other Internet fronts – notably Internet commerce. In February 1995, as a merchant acquirer, Wells Fargo was the first bank to provide merchants with a secure system for Internet credit card payments using a system from Cybercash Inc. In December 1996, Wells Fargo provided an Internet payment solution based on the Secure Electronic Transaction specification, using its branded vPOS merchant software from VeriFone Inc. It also issues branded SET-compliant digital certificates to merchants, using technology supplied by GTE Corp.

The *Wall Street Journal*

In April 1996, Dow Jones & Company launched the *Wall Street Journal* (*WSJ*) Interactive Journal (http://wsj.com). Produced by a dedicated 24-hour staff of more than thirty-five editors and other news professionals in the *WSJ*'s New York newsroom, the Interactive Journal provides continuously updated coverage of the full spectrum of business, including corporate news, financial markets, personal finance, technology, law and marketing. Its 50,000 pages of information and news also provide political and economic coverage combined with updated sports and weather reports. The Interactive and print edition teams are co-located and cooperate closely over copy. In the autumn of 1996, the *WSJ* began charging for its electronic journal, securing 50,000 subscriptions by the end of that year. By June 1997 this had risen to over 100,000, generating nearly 20 million hits a week.

The Interactive Journal provides breaking coverage of news from more than 1,000 Dow Jones reporters based around the world, includes stories from the daily print edition and enhances stories with in-depth background information and supporting documents. Thus, for example, the Interactive Journal provides instant access to news from European and Asian markets, special reports on Internet trends, in-depth reports on companies and the early availability of the print edition's next day's stories. The majority of its subscribers are US-based but with a healthy international readership: 20 per cent of international customers are Canadian, 14 per cent Japanese, 10 per cent British with 5.7 per cent based in Hong Kong, 4.9 per cent in Australia and 4.6 per cent in Germany.

In innovation terms, the Interactive Journal was preceded by the Money & Investing Update, launched in July 1995, and by Briefing Books added in September 1995. The latter added a new level of analysis and research capabilities to the Update, with hyperlinks that furnished detailed corporate and financial information, including one-year stock performance graphs, on any of more than 9,000 public companies mentioned within articles. It aimed to capture the advantages of an interactive medium: immediacy of broadcast, for example with news breaking stories updated every fifteen minutes if appropriate; 'depth' of print, enabling readers to 'dig deep' behind a story to understand the broad market context; and automatic links to sources of rich background details. The Interactive Journal has embodied such features.

Among the Interactive Journal features announced in 1997 was the Personal Journal News Alert and the Dow Jones News/Retrieval Publications Library. The former enables Interactive subscribers to receive automatic delivery of the top five headlines and stories meeting their customer profiles. Effectively, they can track only the news that is most important to them by designing their own personal news portfolio and can monitor their own personalised investment portfolio. Subscribers are warned of the arrival of new stories with an alert box that appears on their computer screens, even if they are not using a Web application at the time. The News Alert makes use of the BackWeb client application from BackWeb Technologies Inc.

As of autumn 1997, the large Dow Jones News/Retrieval Publications Library enables Interactive subscribers to search current and past articles from more than 3,700 newspapers, magazines and business-news sources. Subscribers may do unlimited searching and read headlines at no additional charge, while articles may be viewed for a cost of $2.95 each.

Features designated as 'cool stuff' on the Web site include the following: a Small Business Suite offering a broad range of small-business and home-office coverage grouped into one area; special reports on breaking news events, for example, Supreme Court rulings, the TWA disaster and the Oklahoma bombing (where appropriate these are indexed from the print edition under the latter's Journal Links); Voices, a forum for readers to exchange views on news events; and Images, where images are captured and created to complement news coverage. Images may also create news in their own right as, for example, with the Interactive Journal's first Virtual Gallery which presented the photographer Annie Leibovitz's portraits of Olympic athletes accompanied by a short audio description.

One of the unique features of the Interactive Journal is its ability to deliver breaking news stories by virtue of the immediacy of the medium. For example, in March 1997, Interactive Journal readers got an advance on Warren Buffett's much-anticipated annual letter to Berkshire Hathaway shareholders, when an editor obtained early access to the letter via its posting on the Berkshire Hathaway Web site. The Interactive Journal quickly notified subscribers by e-mail and posted a story about the letter's implications for investors. In April 1997, Apex Global Information Services, operator of a key element of the Internet's infrastructure, suffered 'a concentrated and systematic attack' on its network. Interactive Journal editors learned of the hacker attack, and resulting service outrage, through heated, late-night user-group messages on Usenet. A story was posted just a few hours later, informing readers of the situation and the significance of the attack.

The Interactive Journal is among the industry's first Web publishing ventures to seek subscription revenue from readers. The subscription rate is $49 annually, with subscribers to any edition of the print *Wall Street Journal* paying a lower rate of $29 annually. The team includes a staff of editors, designers, programmers and business managers, with titles such as Editor, Managing Editor, Creative Designer, Web Master, Business Director, Advertising Manager, and Technical Director. For example, the role of the Advertising Manager includes tailoring creative ad programmes to meet the unique needs of each advertiser, providing solid tracking and measurement, and leveraging interactive Web technology to support advertising programmes, while the Technical Director is responsible for the architecture, design, implementation, deployment and support of the Interactive Journal systems and networks.

ONLINE ENTREPRENEURS

Electronic Share Information (ESI)

Founded in 1993 by Hermann Hauser of Acorn Computers, ESI offers a wide range of investment services with online dealing facility. The aim is to offer private investors easy, instantaneous access to the type of online private information and financial services previously available only to major investing institutions. ESI is privately funded and is wholly independent, not being owned, funded or influenced by any financial services organisation.

ESI launched its interactive online share price information service, ESIQuote, in September 1995. On registration, free ESI services include ESIQuote Free and ESITrust – Unit Trust Prices. Subscription services include ESIQuote Silver – Real-time; ESIQuote Bronze; ESIData – Data downloads; and ESIQuote CompuServe. ESI (http://www.esi.co.uk) offers investors real-time share prices, portfolio management, and an online trading gateway. Subscriptions are handled by direct debit or card authority, collected monthly, with client money being deposited with brokers offline. ESI provides its customers with access to comprehensive information on stocks and shares, day and night, seven days a week. Customers can manage and value their portfolio, call up share prices in real-time, form valuations and look up company news, analytical information and forecasts. UK listed shares can be bought and sold over the Internet.

As of August 1997, ESI provided prices on over 4,000 listings of shares, gilts, bonds, international stock and AIM companies, and on over 2,500 unit trusts. This service offers private investors access to a wide array of investment information including portfolio management, charting, news, company financials, stockwatch five-year price histories and real-time prices from the London Stock Exchange. As of August 1997, ESI had over 100,000 registered users; over 300 new users registering each day; 3,000 different users accessing the site each weekday; and approximately four million 'hits' (accesses to the site) a week. Approximately 75 per cent of users are British residents and 25 per cent are British expatriates or non-Brits. Customers appear to prefer the anonymity of the procedure, its rapid execution and the economies which the service offers.

In May 1997, ESI announced ESIOption – the first Internet service to provide option prices from LIFFE (London International Financial Futures and Options Exchange). ESIOption lists periodic prices for all LIFFE equity options and for the FTSE 100 Index option as a free service. The prices are offered as periodic snap-shots of the market, updated every fifteen minutes. ESIOption is the latest service on the ESI personal finance web site which features stock prices from the London Stock Exchange, UK unit trust prices, company data, real-time news, portfolio management, charting facilities, along with access to online dealing services from ShareLink, Stocktrade, Fleming Luxembourg and Union CAL.

Dealing & Equity Options on the Net (DEON), the first UK equity dealing service on the Internet, was announced by ESI in February 1997 and offered by them in partnership with Union CAL Ltd. DEON, commissioned by Union CAL Ltd and implemented by ESI, provides investors with access to up-to-date information on the equity options market and other world markets including derivatives and foreign exchange. DEON is unique in that it offers all traditional trading services, including equity prices, research, option facilities and dealing (during LIFFE market hours) at any time, day or night.

Prior to DEON, ESI announced its partnership with Fleming Fund Management (Luxembourg) in December 1996. This partnership led to the first pan-European Internet dealing service for investment funds, allowing customers to open an account via the Web and proceed to buy, switch or sell from the Fleming Flagship Fund. The dealing service provides information on all offshore funds in the Fleming Flagship range including product information, daily fund prices, fund performance information, daily and weekly market overviews and fund managers' reports in English, German and Italian.

Firefly

Originating from Massachusetts Institute of Technology's Media Lab, Firefly Networks Inc., previously Agents Inc., was incorporated in March 1995 and began the deployment of a proprietary artificial intelligence, or 'agent' technology, to the Web in the form of Firefly. In early 1996, the company launched the Firefly site (http://www.firefly.com) for people seeking personalised music and movie recommendations. The service offers members a variety of features, initially including music reviews, audio samples, chat rooms, music recommendations which match their tastes, personal home pages and Flypaper, an online magazine. Using the software, customers could find other people within the Firefly community who shared their tastes and to whom they could communicate through real-time chat or exchange private messages or 'whispers' in one-to-one messaging.

Word of mouth – one of the most powerful influences on customer buying decisions – is usually limited to a circle of immediate friends, relatives and colleagues, but US Cambridge-based, Firefly Networks Inc. found a way to expand that valued group using their proprietary Internet-based software. It works like this. Visitors to the site assign themselves an alias and begin to register their likes and dislikes in movies and music. The company's agent software, called Firefly Passports, is made available free to customers who agree to fill out surveys and rank Web sites as they surf the Internet. The data collected creates a customer profile. Software programs known as intelligent agents take over, sifting through similar lists logged by other users, locating 'nearest psychological neighbours' and using that information to recommend to the customer other music CDs and films, free of charge.

To provide the ability to purchase recommended products online, Firefly entered into strategic relationships with a variety of entertainment, media and merchandise companies including Newbury Comics, a music retailer which fulfils music CD orders placed with Firefly; The All Music Guide, a reference guide with reviews of musical recordings; HitsWorld, suppliers of the Internet Music Charts; Ogilvy & Mather, a digital communications and marketing company; and Muzak's Enso Audio Imaging Division, which provides audio and music support to businesses on the Internet.

Firefly has since expanded into recommending movies in addition to music. The movie area draws from The All Movie Guide, a definitive reference guide with reviews of thousands of movies, and features reviews, plot synopses, cast lists and links to actors containing filmography, biographies and movie facts. Members can rate and review movies just as they rate music. The more a member rates albums and movies, the more personalised Firefly's recommendations become. Initially, it is focusing on music and movies, but over time, Firefly plans to expand into mutual funds, restaurants and books. It also uses the information it has about individual preferences to showcase its advertisers' banners in front of those most likely to be interested.

Firefly offers the ability to gather inexpensively customer data that goes beyond standard demographics based on zip codes, ages and gender. Advertisers are able to construct targeted messages to Firefly customers based on several criteria, including detailed entertainment preferences and electronic lifestyle features. Once the profile of the target consumer has been determined by the marketer and the banners created, Firefly's technology ensures each message is delivered to the appropriate individuals.

Thus the strategic intention behind Firefly's software is to provide a tool which can zero in on groups with well-defined preferences: it can provide marketers with an electronic and customised pitch at a fraction of the cost of more traditional direct-marketing programs. It's a marketer's nirvana – a means to micro-target a highly-defined relevant customer segment at low cost.

Firefly is one of the companies at the forefront of the Web's movement towards personalisation, accountability and effectiveness, for consumers and marketers alike. While some people have fears about divulging the level of detailed personal information which Firefly requires, customers know that this is a *quid pro quo* for a free service prior to signing up for their Firefly Passport. Moreover, the company strives to safeguard individual privacy and, at the same time, facilitate effective micro-targeted database marketing. By not asking for users' names or addresses, Firefly guarantees to maintain the privacy and integrity of information about its user base. It has also engaged the auditing firm of Coopers and Lybrand to evaluate its privacy procedures regularly.

In addition to receiving personalised recommendations, Firefly customers also have the ability to review advertising banners according to how successful marketers have been in creatively targeting their messages. Consumers have the opportunity to rate an album or movie on the Firefly Web site. This allows advertisers both a quantitative and qualitative measurement – fairly unusual not only for advertising on the Web but for broadcast media as well.

Firefly investors include Japanese software company Softbank Corp., Dun & Bradstreet, Trident Capital, venture capital firm Atlas Ventures and Merrill Lynch: the company has raised $18 million in venture capital funding since its start. CEO Nicholas Grouf says advertising has provided the startup with small but growing revenues, now from advertisers including MCI, Honda Motor, MasterCard, AT&T and Columbia Records, but he views the popular site primarily as a showcase for the company's agent technology.

In August 1996, Firefly started to move away from being a Web site deploying its own proprietary software agents to assuming the role of a company that licenses its technology. This change of emphasis was signalled in February 1997 with Firefly's acquisition of NetAngels, a developer of agent applications. Among the first to sign up to a software licence were other Internet businesses including Reuters New Media, Yahoo!, and Ziff-Davis Publishing Co's ZDNet: they were followed by AOL Greenhouse and Barnes & Noble Inc. Firefly is licensing a tool which enables traders and retailers to deliver highly targeted advertising, and companies to build affinity groups around their brand. The suite of software tools can be applied to any electronic network – whether it's an Internet, an intranet, or a broadband or mobile network.

Internet Bookshop

The Internet Bookshop, founded in 1993, has no physical high street presence but exists entirely on the Internet. The Bookshop (http://www.bookshop.co.uk) 'stocks' approximately one million books and operates a 24-hour ordering service plus its own order fulfilment service.

Compared to a traditional high street bookshop, the Internet Bookshop enjoys many competitive advantages. It does not have to pay the overheads associated with a high-street presence, the only physical space required being for its fulfilment operation and associated support services. No stock is held on site, apart from those books that are being processed for dispatch. Staff requirements are limited to customer support, marketing, finance, fulfilment and technical services: there is no need for dedicated retail sales staff. The Bookshop can therefore absorb further increases in sales volumes without a corresponding rise in costs. The company has experienced rapid growth rates. Compound growth in terms of sales volumes averaged approximately 20 per cent monthly in the period from May to December 1996, with orders of approximately 7,500 books in January 1997.

Security is achieved by the use of a secure server system which encrypts credit card details online. The majority of customers use this method to give these details, whilst others choose to give details verbally or by fax. Throughout order processing, customers are frequently updated on the status of their order through the use of automatically generated e-mail messages and through status-checking facilities built into the site. This arrangement allows for a greater degree of customer interaction than would normally be the case for a physical retailer. This rapport is enhanced by the e-mailing of a regular newsletter to the Bookshop's customer database. Since it started trading, 29,000 people have joined the Bookshop's mailing list.

The front screen of the Internet Bookshop is effectively its most expensive 'real estate'. As in all sites, this electronic 'foyer' or 'store-front' is critical in determining how customers will react to the site. Thus the intellectual software assets implicit in its design represent one of the company's most critical investments. This first screen not only sets the tone and feel of the Bookshop but is one of the primary vehicles for orientating customers. It provides a mechanism for electronic searching and order placing, plus a source of related editorial and literary information. By this means it has sold some rather bizarre titles including *Illustrated Gay Wrestling*, *An Illustrated History of Plastics* (collectors' edition); and *Tattoos and Body Art*.

Much of the 'atmosphere' of the Bookshop is captured in the design of the front screen or 'store-front'. It provides links to other screens ('shop areas') covering the top 100 selling titles, publishers' sites, an author area, the book of the month feature, the British Book Awards arena, and publisher, customer and author comments. For example, in early May 1997, the Bookshop featured Michael Ondaatje's *The English Patient* as the book of the month; an Internet knowledge competition; a feature on the Principles of Marketing with a sample chapter online; *The Spirit Level* – the 1997 Whitbread Winner; *Longitude* – an award winning book which 'does the impossible and makes horology sexy'; and, Dean Koontz's *Sole Survivor* – the new novel from the international best seller of *Mr Murder*, *Winter Moon*, and *Dark Rivers of the Heart*.

The Bookshop also provides an order status enquiry facility, an account maintenance check, and a frequently-asked-questions customer 'rapport area'. A key new departure in 1997 was the creation of 'department floors' and the facility to search for a book using the company's hierarchically structured 'departments' and 'shelves'. Business, professional and academic users account for approximately 58 per cent of customers. Non-fiction titles, mainly of an academic or professional nature, have accounted for approximately 70 per cent of the titles sold by the company so far, the remainder being made up of mainstream fiction titles.

In many countries UK-published books are not readily available, and where they are, the mark-up charged by importers can be prohibitive and delays in obtaining books can be significant. Being located on the Internet, the Bookshop is able to offer its international client base books at UK prices. Approximately 79 per cent of sales go abroad and books are dispatched to approximately 70 countries every month. Marketing foreign language books also means that the company will be able to enter other language markets such as Spanish, French and German, leading to exposure to markets in South America as well as Europe.

Peapod

Peapod, founded in 1989, with headquarters in Skokie, Illinois, is the largest interactive online grocery shopping and delivery service in the USA. The company was created by Andrew and Thomas Parkinson working with a small core of computer specialists. They each have a stake in the company with the rest of the company being owned by venture capital groups and WPP, the advertising group. Peapod's online service is currently accessible via direct dial-up and the Internet (http://www.peapod.com). It is a third-party fulfilment company offering a shopping and delivery service though relationships with stores including Jewel Food Stores in Chicago, Safeway in San Francisco and San Jose, Kroger in Columbus, Stop & Shop in Boston, Randalls in Houston, Bruno's in Atlanta, and serves approximately 50,000 members (customers). The Stop & Shop Supermarket Company, for example, is New England's largest supermarket chain, operates 186 supermarkets including 134 superstores in Connecticut, Massachusetts, New York and Rhode Island.

It also provides one of the only operational forums for executing one-to-one interactive marketing at the point-of-purchase and online product research. In June 1997, Peapod announced its initial public offering of shares on the American stock exchange, Nasdaq. Proceeds of the offering will be used to expand into new geographical markets and for further penetration of existing markets and other corporate developments. Peapod's financial backers include Ameritech, Tribune Co., EOS Partners, and Dispatch Interactive Television Inc.

Monthly membership of Peapod is $6.95, which includes three hours of online shopping time and Internet e-mail access. Shopping, packing and delivery charges are $4.95 per order plus 5 per cent of the grocery total. Peapod members in the Boston area, for instance, have access to a database of more than 20,000 items sold at Stop & Shop. Members have the opportunity to make comments on their electronic order form, for example, instructing their 'surrogate shoppers' to choose products in a certain condition (for example, degree of ripeness of bananas) or meeting certain specifications (for example, organic foods with Soil Association labelling). Grocery orders can be placed 24-hours a day, seven days a week, and same-day delivery is possible if the order is placed three hours in advance of the desired 90-minute delivery time slot. Alternatively, 'pinpoint' delivery, that is, within a 30-minute window, can be selected for a small additional charge. Groceries are delivered in temperature-controlled coolers and crush-proof bins. Payment for delivery can be made by cheque, credit or debit card, or Peapod Electronic Payment.

Customers download software from the Peapod Web site or order it through calling the Peapod freefone number. The computer software links customers to the Peapod database of merchandise and offers four methods of shopping: shopping by personal list (stored on the customer's hard drive for frequently ordered items); shop by aisle (an icon representation of the various grocery departments); find item (a keyword search, for example, for a specific product or brand); or, shop by last order. Peapod added the Internet as an access point to its dial-up network service in June 1996. Clients (sponsors) include companies such as Ralston Purina Co., Kraft Foods Inc., M&M Mars, Nestlé Food Co., Ore-Ida Foods and Bristol-Myres Squibb Co.

PhotoDisc

PhotoDisc, a digital photoshop, was the first company to publish royalty-free digital stock photography on multimedia CD (CD-ROM). It was founded by Chairman and CEO Mark Torrance, a licensing expert who had previously launched music companies, Muzak and Yesco. His aim was to provide communications professionals with an easier, more cost-effective way to acquire high quality images. In fulfilling that aim, the company sells images on disc and via the Internet to customers ranging from designers, advertising agencies and new media consultancies to publishers, broadcasting companies and marketing communications staff. PhotoDisc merged with Getty Communications (now Getty Images) in September 1997.

PhotoDisc was established in 1991, with its first CD product issued in January 1992, and launched its commercial Web site (http://www.photodisc.com) in October 1995. The company has its headquarters in Seattle, with offices in London, Hamburg, Sydney and New York, and an outsourced European customer service facility in Scotland.

As at January 1997, the PhotoDisc collection comprised more

than 50,000 images with approximately 2,000 new ones being added every month. Approximately 20,000 of these images are available in the company's CD-ROM product line. All images can be found on the company's Web site and the majority of new images are available via the site exclusively. In terms of visitors to the site – or site traffic – there are over 3,000 user sessions per day. Twelve per cent of the volume is generated by companies in sixty-five different countries outside the States. Web sales exceed $500,000 per month. PhotoDisc was a pioneer in offering secure online purchasing of print-ready images using RSA encryption; in building a site using OneServer software; in implementing Virage visual search software; in providing credit card authorisation in real time; and in offering Shockwave animated images.

PhotoDisc is founded on licensing principles, so photographers lease both PhotoDisc and its customers the right to use their images. Low resolution versions are available for comping purposes, while higher resolution images are sold in different file sizes for use in the finished design. Single low and high resolution images can be bought and downloaded from the company's Web site which carries the entire image range. High resolution images are offered on themed CD-ROM volumes with built in browsers, with each disc containing between 100 and 400 images. All images are both Mac and Windows compatible. Once the right image has been sourced, the customer chooses the required resolution and either buys the image/s in real time using Cybercash (a highly secure online payment transaction method) or phones PhotoDisc with their credit card details to set up an image account. The image/s can then be downloaded.

As an indicator of its growth, the company took on its hundredth employee in April 1996 and is aiming to employ 296 staff worldwide by the end of 1997. Sales have been doubling annually since the company's inception, rising to a turnover of more than $25 million in 1996. In that year, 10 per cent of business revenues were generated via the Net. The company plans to increase this to 50 per cent of revenues by the year 2000. Sales outside the USA made up 25 per cent of the company's 1996 total revenue, while worldwide Web sales contributed 20 per cent to the total.

The purpose of the Web site is to allow customers to search quickly and efficiently through the 50,000-plus image collection, and to buy and download the images they need 24 hours a day, seven days a week. The site also provides value added information (magazines 'In the Loupe' for photographers and 'Design Mind' for designers, plus company information) and a feedback loop for customers. The software technology currently used on the site includes: an Oracle database; CONNECT OneServer (acts as the 'glue' on top of Oracle); Cybercash/Verisign (for encryption of credit card details); a combination of Fulcrum, Erli and Virage search technologies (giving combined keyword and concept based searches), enabling creative professionals to search for images intuitively and visually using criteria such as colour, texture, structure and composition, as well as keywords and natural language strings. The hardware used is a mix of Sun and NT servers. By June 1997, $2 million had been spent on building the site.

Key PhotoDisc photographers include Doug Menuez, Nick Koudis, Mark Downey, Bruce Heinemann, Keith Brofsky, Lawrence Lawry and Adam Crowley. Sales revenue is shared with photographers through royalties, which are paid based on images sold both online and through disc products. As PhotoDisc licenses images from its photographers, it is the photographers who retain all copyright to their images. PhotoDisc also uses watermarks on comping images, where appropriate, to provide a visual deterrent and reminder of rights obligations.

Salon

Salon (http://www.salonmagazine.com) is an original content Internet magazine covering books, arts and ideas. Founded in November 1995 by David Talbot, former Arts and Features Editor at the *San Francisco Examiner*, Salon received major financing from Adobe Systems and Hambrecht & Quist. Since its launch, it has grown from a bimonthly literary e-zine into a highbrow, high-volume entertainment daily with a monthly page view count of two million. It describes itself as a smart, elegant Web-based magazine that appeals to the digital intelligentsia and neophytes alike.

In addition to regular contributions by its feature writers, Salon includes a number of regular departments – Media Circus; The Salon Interview; Newsreal; Wanderlust; Table Talk Forum; 21st; Taste; Sneak Peeks; and Sharps & Flats. Salon's book section, Sneak Peeks, and its music section, Sharps & Flats, are sponsored by Borders Books and Music, a national US retailer with over

170 outlets. According to the Salon site, Media Circus is a funny and trenchant coverage of the world of media and entertainment, separating the weird from the worthy in this daily column on the personalities and trends that are shaping communications in the 1990s.

The Salon Interview provides provocative, intimate conversations with a range of cultural personalities including authors, film-makers and performers. More than eighty in-depth interviews have appeared to date in the magazine, including: John le Carré, Amy Tan, Oliver Stone, Salman Rushdie, Tony Kushner and Alice Walker.

Salon describes Table Talk Forum as a lively conversation at party which never stops. With 1,500 topics being discussed, including digital culture, books, politics, personal life, and entertainment, Table Talk is one of the most popular interactive reader conferencing areas on the Web. Links from Salon's feature stories help stimulate discussion and debate.

Readership statistics can be summarised thus: more than 3.8 million 'page views' in July 1997, 54,000 Table Talk participants, and 35,000 registered newsletter recipients. Readers of Salon are distinctive among Internet users. According to recent research, they are upscale, educated, evenly divided between the genders and include professionals in communications, education, computers, consulting etc.

The opportunities for correspondence, analysis, review and rapport which an electronic world presents are exemplified by Salon's travel department, Wanderlust. Each week the Wanderlust cover story highlights one destination with in-depth, personal explorations and evocations by such writers as Jan Morris, Isabel Allende, Peter Mayle, Pico Iyer and Simon Winchester. The stories are accompanied by 'savvy' service information and linked directly to the reader forum. In On the Road, editor Donald George provides a reflective introduction to the Wanderlust fare or a dispatch from his own peripatetic travels.

Postmark, one of Wanderlust's editorial sections, presents a local writer's up-to-the-minute report of his or her hometown's current passions and peccadilloes, whether it's a new restaurant, a fad, a political intrigue or an entertainment sensation. Another section, Passages, features a weekly excerpt from a notable new travel book, accompanied by an interview with the author, and an icon to fast forward you to the merchandise order screen. In the Readers' Tip section seasoned travellers share their favourite tips and most recent discoveries.

Salon has recently hired Marc Wernick, VP of Marketing and Business Development, whose background includes brand management at P&G, and strategic planning at McKinsley & Co., Grey Entertainment and Ogilvy and Mather Direct. In addition to developing the Salon brand on and off the Web, Marc Wernick will be active in pursuing Salon's plans to develop an affinity programme, e-commerce, e-education and content syndication.

Security First Network Bank

Security First Network Bank (http://www.sfnb.com) started life as a division of Cardinal Bancshares, a public company traded on the NASDAQ with headquarters in Lexington, Kentucky. SFNB was then spun off to become one of the pioneers in electronic banking on the Internet. The Bank has no physical high street presence except for a single city office in Peachtree Road, Atlanta, Georgia, USA.

SFNB opened its virtual doors to the public in October 1995 offering, at that point, only basic cheque accounts. Since then, it has introduced certificates of deposit, money market accounts, interest checking and basic saving accounts with plans to add a brokerage department, a loan department, a basic business cheque account and an SFNB Visa Credit Card. Its asset size in June 1997 was $41 million. The Bank's goal is to offer the same full range of products and services as conventional 'bricks and mortar' banks. At the moment, though, there are limitations on its service because, for instance, the technology behind digital watermarking, digital signatures and digital thumb-prints is not yet operational. Cash deposits cannot be made and customers must rely on sending (physical) cheques in the (physical) post.

The Bank operates from its single office with only a small staff. The low operating cost enables it to offer a competitive 5.5 per cent interest rate (the US average is 3.5 per cent) making it an attractive proposition to prospective customers. It is able to handle its customers' deposits by any one of six methods: direct deposit of payroll, federal or state cheques; wire transfer; the automated clearing house transfer; US Mail or other trusted courier, for example, FedEx, DHL, UPS Red Label; by using the Bank's ATM in Atlanta; or, finally, by a visit to the Bank's headquarters in Atlanta. Customers pay bills and write cheques electronically on their PC and accounts are updated at any point, twenty-four hours a day.

The level of security and encryption technology employed by SFNB is, as is necessary, exceptionally high. SFNB operates on Five Paces Virtual Bank Manager software, which includes security technologies developed by SecureWare Inc., Atlanta (who provided the US Department of Defense with encryption technology used, among other purposes, to protect the flight plans of Stealth bombers and Tomahawk cruise missiles from unwanted intrusion), in conjunction with Hewlett Packard, Palo Alto, California. These meet the US National Computer Security Center criteria for B-1 level security, this being the highest security level attainable for commercial information systems. The security system is built upon a multilevel security platform which incorporates encryption technologies to protect data and ensure privacy as information travels over open networks; firewalls and filtering routers limit access to the system from external networks; and the B-1 level operating system provides strong access controls that create virtual lock-boxes for each customer, protecting against unauthorised tampering with customers' private account information. This security is the digital equivalent of armoured cars, security guards and vaults in conventional banking. SFNB has an arrangement to reimburse 100 per cent of customers' funds should funds be removed from that customer's account without their authorisation, provided it is within the bank's control.

SSEYO

SSEYO is an Internet music software development and music publishing company. It specialises in 'generative' music and sound environments. Through its Koan software product range, developed over the last seven years, its Koan content and the SSEYO KoanMusic Engine (SKME) for real-time music generation, it has established an international reputation, especially for its Internet-based music solutions and its music creativity tools.

The company's first product, Koan Plus V1.0, was released in the autumn of 1994 and the Koan range was further expanded in November 1995 with the release of Koan Pro V1.0 and then by Koan X – a drag 'n' mix generative music powertool for the consumer market – in December 1996. Koan X is available in three versions – Platinum, Gold and Silver – with varying features and capabilities. This PC software simplifies the creation of KoanMusic by employing drag-and-drop capabilities along with a varied selection of pre-authored generative musical templates. KoanMusic is low bandwidth, interactive and MIDI (Musical Instrument Digital Interface) based. The experimental, non-looping and personal nature of music and sound the SKME generates is well suited to Web sites, 3-D Web virtual worlds, gaming and situations where fresh, interactive music or sound content is required. In 1997, SSEYO launched MIKE (Massively Interactive Koan Experience) which allows real-time control over 200 Koan parameters from a Web page using Microsoft's VBScript or Netscape's JavaScript.

Koan X Silver is freely available from the company's Web site (http://www.sseyo.com). The more advanced Koan X Gold and Platinum versions are available for electronic purchase and download via the Web site. There are over 100 templates available in the Platinum version, divided into six categories including Loops, Ambient, Arpeggio, Base, Drums and Orchestral. The templates are collections of over 200 parameters or 'seed' values that are created by Koan artists using Koan Pro. As artists create the templates it means users do not need to understand the complexities and intricacies of the Koan system in order to be able to generate an infinite stream of music. Recognising that content is a key component, Koan X has been designed as an expandable system and further packs of templates are available.

Like Microsoft and Netscape, SSEYO has adopted the policy of providing free 'sample' versions of their latest releases to users on the Net. Should they wish to, these users can then purchase the more advanced versions which provide added value. SSEYO is aiming to license its Koan technology and is building strategic relationships with companies like Microsoft, Netscape, Creative Labs, Emu and Yamaha. It is also working with BT Laboratories in its 'Shared Space' project which explores the linkages between objects in a virtual environment and KoanMusic.

Koan authoring tools enable everyone with a multimedia PC and sound card to make contemporary music from the desktop, quickly and easily. Prospective users range from musicians creating personal compositions to Web site developers improving and creating sites with music. SSEYO itself launched the KoanMusic title 'Niskala' by Jamuud of Loop Guru in June 1997. It is a CD-ROM which includes Koan player software, 27 Koan pieces specially written for one of the Creative Lab sound cards together with Jamuud's recordings of selected, treated and mixed studio 'cuts' of a number of the Koan pieces. Also Koan Pro, SSEYO's flagship product, was used by Brian Eno, the celebrated avant garde music producer, to create the twelve Koan pieces on 'Generative Music 1', another KoanMusic title published by SSEYO in May 1996. None of the twelve pieces will ever play the same twice.

In essence, instead of having to specify exactly what notes are played, Koan software allows people to 'grow' music by specifying certain parameters and then letting the computer improvise according to various rules. Whenever a Koan piece is played, the SKME interprets the parameter settings contained within the Koan 'piece' to compose in real-time the ensuing KoanMusic. The KoanMusic occurs as the SKME sends out MIDI information to the sound card or sound module which then produces the sounds. The SKME can give performances that are different each time, based on the settings of over 200 musical variables. At the core of KoanMusic lies the control of the sound palette, the music rules, any 'seed' patterns and the inter-relationships between the various components in the Koan piece. The music changes from a predicted pattern to totally unexpected combinations of timbre, rhythm, scale and harmonies. Like screensavers, which contain a set of rules that determine how visual shapes move about a screen in a largely random manner, generative music can let the computer itself decide the sequence and movements of 'sound shapes'. Thus rather than creating music from scratch, SSEYO's Koan software uses a generative music system to create constantly evolving musical patterns.

SSEYO uses Internet service provider UUNET's commercial online software to enable selection, purchasing and distribution of its software and content in real-time. This enables SSEYO to reach a global customer base. Musicians, games developers, creative Internet users and Website developers worldwide can buy music software programs directly off the Internet and use them immediately. The Bureau provides secure, straight-through transactions with none of the distribution and stockholding costs or inventory risks associated with other channels. Online selling is one channel in SSEYO's multi-channel distribution strategy allowing the company to match attractive customer segments who are advanced computer users with the channel that best suits their needs.

Travelocity

Travelocity is a one-stop travel site (http://www.travelocity.com) and is the project of Sabre Interactive, a leading provider of online travel reservations services. Elements of the content are provided by Worldview Systems Corporation, a publisher of interactive and online destination information.

As of autumn 1997, Sabre Interactive, through the Travelocity site, offered schedules for more than 700 airlines; reservations and tickets for more than 400 airlines; and reservation and purchase capability for more than 35,000 hotels and more than 50 car-rental companies. Worldwide Systems provides an online travel guide to more than 22,000 destinations, with in-depth profiles and current activities information for more than 200 featured destinations. The database can be searched by keyword, phrase, destination or interest. The Web software can be set to search automatically for the lowest fare available between multiple cities and to display the three lowest-cost itineraries. Travelocity provides a customer service centre to meet the needs of online travel shoppers which is available on a freefone number. Through the site a potential traveller has access to approximately 1,700 maps, photos, video clips and sound clips.

Aside from travel reservation as such, Travelocity carries details on restaurants, museums, B&B facilities, theatres, dance and music performances, condominiums, golf courses, hotels, exhibits, shows and festivals. There is also a merchandise area which provides, for example, Merchant Roster, a list of merchants providing innovative travel products. Featured news items include 'today's discounts', 'travel watch' for information on manoeuvring round new places; and a 'fare-watcher service' which provides an 'electronic eye' on low fares and can monitor up to five separate round-trips if requested.

The 'Today's Lowest Fares' section provides a directory on the homepage which highlights the lowest fares for multiple flights from the fourteen most popular cities booked by Travelocity customers. A direct link is provided to the Travelocity Three

Best Itineraries section for immediate booking. Airfare comparisons are updated three times daily to ensure that the lowest fares are shown. An animated graphic displays the fares with the greatest price reductions.

Another section, Points of View, provides Chat & Forums (enabling browsers to touch base with fellow travellers on a broad range of travel topics), Travelive (regularly scheduled live chats and conferences with travel experts), Travels with Elgy (columnist Elgy Gillespie sharing her perspective on the world), Worldviews (features on places and people, travels and trends around the world), Savvy Traveler (syndicated journalist Peter S. Greenberg offers tips and wisdom to the frequent traveller), Spotlight (special feature profile of a destination or topic of the month), and Fun & Games (an entertainment area to challenge the wits of the travel-savvy).

Under the section Travelocity Trivia in May 1997, the site promoted an Australian outback hiking vacation following Aboriginal trails inviting the browser to check out Travelocity's tips for tours and trips in Melbourne and find Dreamtime Outback Safaris. This Safaris company can take the traveller on, quote, 'a camping trip with members of the Parrkindji tribe in the land of Mungo, a tribal meeting place for thousands of years', or set customers up with an Aboriginal guide for a tour through the mountains of Victoria's High Country. It also poses hypothetical situations like, for instance, 'need to make a multi-stop starting in Seattle, travelling to Cleveland and Louisville, then returning to Seattle?' It then advertises its FlightFinder feature which can automatically search through up to 900 options and locate the lowest priced itinerary between, in this case, the three cities.

Also under Travelocity Trivia, with a paragraph headed Computer Culture, it invites the customer to check out Travelocity's Business Information section before setting off for a business trip. This includes information, amongst other things, on where to rent a laptop in Istanbul if the traveller 'dies of culture shock'. It further invites the browser to check the Foreign Protocol Etiquette listings to learn that while there you should dress conservatively and keep your feet on the ground because 'to show the soles of your shoes to anyone is considered very insulting'.

The Sabre computer reservation system which powers Travelocity handles more than 30 per cent of the world's airline reservations booked through global reservation systems – more than 300 million trip itineraries each year. Sabre Interactive's Silicon Graphics Inc., WebForce Challenge servers and Worldview System's Sun Microsystems SPARC servers provide the hardware and computing power for Travelocity.

Virtual Vineyards

Virtual Vineyards offers premium wine from small, limited production wineries – including lesser known artisan producers – in California and Europe and speciality foods from around the world. The company's products are to be found in over 1,500 pages of web content describing wineries, wines and cuisine (http://www.virtualvin.com). Since 1995, the company has raised more than $5 million in private investment from sources that include Alpine Technology, Applied Technology Ventures, and Bayview Fund and Broderbund Software. The company is known for both its distinctive, hard-to-find offerings and for its proprietor, Master Sommelier Peter Granoff, who has been a professional wine buyer for more than fifteen years.

Products are shipped to both the United States and international destinations, except where local law restrictions apply, from a temperature-controlled warehouse in the Napa Valley. Ground shipment is used for delivery to states west of the Rockies and second-day air delivery to other locations. As of June 1997, the company carried hundreds of products from over eighty California wineries, a small but growing number of European wineries, and from over fifty food producers. Payment options include Visa, MasterCard, American Express, JCB and Cybercash. Online ordering accounts for 98 per cent of orders.

Granoff co-founded Virtual Vineyards with Robert Olson, a Silicon Valley engineering veteran who had spent more than twenty-one years in system design, real-time operating systems, software development, engineering management and marketing. As CEO and president, Olson manages both the technology and business functions, while Granoff is the 'face' and 'spirit' of the company: prior to founding Virtual Vineyards, he was the sommelier and wine director for San Francisco's Square One restaurant. Also a Master Sommelier, Tim Gaiser works with Granoff to select wines for the store's portfolio and respond to customers' questions on food and wine. He has experience of all phases of the wine business – wholesale, retail, winery and restaurant – including stints at Heitz Wine Cellars in the Napa Valley and at the Cypress Club and Bix restaurants in San Francisco.

Virtual Vineyards' management team combines wine and speciality food retailing expertise with the engineering skills needed to develop and maintain a commercial site on the Web. They include the co-founders Peter Granoff, general manager, and Robert Olson, president; chairman Ken Grunzweig; food shop proprietor, Michael Regina; Master Sommelier, Tim Gaiser; and food expert, Louise Fiszer. As of March 1997, the company had sixteen employees. It is located in Palo Alto in California with fulfilment facilities in the Napa Valley, and is independent and privately held. It was founded in late 1994, with the Web site launched in January 1995, the Food Shop added in July 1996 and the Gift Shop in November 1996. Over $2 million has been invested to build the Web site and the underlying systems which support it to provide an integrated fulfilment, inventory and customer service system. The site is in its fifth generation of technology refinement and will be continually improved.

Chapter 6

The Corporate Amoeba

THAT TRANSIENT FEELING

A characteristic of the industrial age was that organisations were able to operate in a comparatively stable environment. Business life, and indeed private life, was stratified, codified, hierarchical, controlled and reasonably predictable, with relatively little social or physical mobility. Relatively long product life-cycles and stable markets made investment in long-term extensive capital projects both financially viable and competitively advantageous. They necessitated, and assumed, large-scale mass production and the construction of equally large-scale factories. These were very physical symbols of a very physical process, and epitomised the material reality of industrial life until the 1950s.

Arguably, the single most identifiable icon of the Industrial Revolution was the factory – a pre-eminently physical manifestation of the large-scale clustering of workers in one location for the duration of their working hours and, indeed, for the duration of their working lives. The economies of scale to be derived from such an arrangement, and the necessity to be sited close to raw materials and sources of power, were so overwhelming that the Industrial Revolution led to immense concentrations of industries and workers in certain such propitious locations – the phenomenon we recognise as urbanisation and the consequential decline of agrarian life. Such a colossal migration was, of course, only made possible by technological innovation and the development of steam power, railroads, canal systems and mechanisation.

The World as Was

Factory life was epitomised by production lines, hierarchical reporting structures and repetitive working patterns. This arrangement was entirely apt when technologies were discrete, the range of products limited and markets, by today's standards, virtually static. Products were manufactured with durability, robustness, repairability and longevity in mind – production and manufacturing functions were developed and refined safe in the knowledge that the technologies and market demands on which they were based would remain stable for relatively long spans of time.

However, in the last fifty years, dramatic increases in social and physical mobility, underpinned and facilitated by the phenomenal growth in communications technology and global transportation, have transformed this stable picture out of all recognition. The environmental stasis, so characteristic of our public and private lives in the industrial era, has been superseded in post-industrial western economies by environmental flow and flux.

When digitally-based technology was first introduced in the manufacturing process in the 1960s it was in the form of process automation. Repetitive production line tasks, hitherto carried out by an army of workers, were automated on a large scale: suddenly robots were the 'in thing' at the cutting edge of industrial innovation. However, this led in the 1970s to the first wave of human corporate fall-out and coincided in the UK with the dramatic shrinking of traditional industries such as coal and steel – those very industries which had given the Industrial Revolution its substance, its atmosphere and its identity.

Moreover, come the 1980s, automation and computerisation had begun to affect the way in which managerial and administrative processes were executed. Middle management employees, previously considered immune to the shrinking effects of computerised technology or information technology (IT), began to bite the redundancy dust. During the 1970s and 1980s, firms began to implement computer-based technology on a wide scale as soon as those technologies had matured to the point at which cost-beneficial applications were feasible.

Such systems tended to be planned in the context of the old company structures and hierarchies – for research and development, production, manufacturing, financial management and marketing.

Technology was not necessarily used to reshape the organisation for competitive advantage but rather to increase its efficiency for finer market performance based on the existing order. Emphasis was placed on automating and codifying old business practices and sustaining old organisational structures; production was still primarily centred on repetitious processing and thus premised on the mindset of the industrial age.

This has now undergone something of a transformation. In the early 1990s, management energy began to focus more on re-engineering the entire structure of the company rather than streamlining existing production processes. The drive for efficiency gave birth to the phenomenon of outsourcing and led to the process of 'de-constructing' and 're-constructing' the business. In order to decide which functions to outsource, senior executives were forced to re-assess the identity of their business in a far more comprehensive way than was necessary, or even desirable, in the past. Which aspects of their business, they asked, could be cost-effectively outsourced and which were so critical to the core business that they had to remain within the shrinking fabric of the organisation?

This has led to a re-examination of the meaning and obligations of employee loyalty and to the creation of other forms of association which are primarily transient and project-based. Thus, globalised competition, industry deregulation and the capability of networked computer systems had forced business executives to question the very structure, purpose and identity of their organisation with a degree of rigour that had never been necessary before. Now, in the late 1990s, the capability of networked technology is forcing executives to re-assess their core functions once more, to contemplate afresh where best to draw the boundaries to their corporate entities. And it is the prospect of 'virtuality' – even looser forms of corporate association – which has brought on this new corporate challenge.

The Road to Virtuality

It is hard to believe that something so minute could be so powerful, but so it is. Microprocessors – computer circuitry squeezed on to slivers of silicon – have given rise to fundamental changes in the basic architecture and defining boundaries of a company. They have given birth to new forms of digital connectivity, and it is that connectivity which is the catalyst towards ever more dynamic organisational forms.

The mainframe computer which dominated the 1960s and 1970s was superseded in the 1970s and 1980s by the mini-computer and networked computer systems; in particular, by what were known as wide area networks (WANs). Mini-computers and WANs signified the beginning of the process of increased miniaturisation and pervasive connectivity. They were, in turn, superseded by the PC and the local area networks (LANs) and by the networked architectures of the 1990s. It is this networked architecture which has been the key catalyst to the blurring of corporate boundaries, the remoulding of corporate processes and the re-sculpting of business functions. It has been the tremendous growth in base technologies, such as microprocessors, memory chips, bandwidth and magnetic/optical storage, which has facilitated the growth of network computing, network intelligence and thus the rise of the network enterprise in the 1990s.

Moreover, it is predicted that these technologies, which underpin connectivity, will continue their dramatic increase in density, performance and price/performance ratio for the next decade at the same pace as in the last. According to Herbert Kircher, managing director of IBM's German operations, 'Most key parameters of these technologies will have improved by a factor of 10 to 100 by the year 2007.'[70] These improvements have created, and will further develop, phenomena such as network computing, multimedia, Internet and intranets; that is, the digital platforms for expanding business presence and creating new business opportunities. It is the advance of silicon semiconductor technology, the emergence of a personal computing standard and the shift to distributed computing and inter-networking which is providing the raw power for the transition to the digital economy.

The rise of the Internet in the early 1990s was highly pivotal in the final transition from local area networks, which were entirely confined within the boundaries of the corporation, to intranets and extranets. The latter extend a company's web of electronic communications, via Internet-like computer links, to its corporate suppliers and business partners. The Internet has turned out to be the key defining architecture in this transition, providing the communication backbone on which companies can connect with their customers, virtually instantaneously and virtually globally. It also provides the open standards and the ubiquity which makes corporate-wide connectivity possible: proprietary-based local and wide area networks, for example, become fully-fledged intranets. This development has lead to the gradual and continuing 'unbundling' of large companies and the creation of what is known as the 'virtual' corporation. We are in the very midst of this unbundling process at the moment.

Thus, during the current post-industrial era – the transitionary period between the industrial economy and the digital economy – new corporate manifestations have taken on an important role in the fabric of business life. The catalysts in this transition have been the ferociously competitive forces of globalisation and the global connectivity afforded by new technology. With re-engineering came downsizing, and with the Internet has come networked communications. In combination these forces have begun to bend and warp the traditional boundaries of a company and have virtually instituted the continuous process of corporate re-engineering. Companies contend that they can no longer afford to carry a large inventory of 'people product' of varying value and quality. They must re-invent themselves as virtual enterprises at the hub of loosely-knit alliances of local companies, all interconnected by global networks. No longer is the shape and substance of an organisation stable, unchanging, physically identifiable and predictable. In order to survive the companies and corporations of today must be willing, amoeba-like, to change and flex as conditions dictate.

The degree to which the flex and change must occur is most evident in organisations at the sharp edge of the cutting edge, those in the high-tech industries. Chapter 4 gave some indication of the way in which new technologies and competitive forces are colliding, giving rise to new competitive dynamics and fresher strategic directions, informed more by lateral thinking than received wisdom.

Variously called organic, networked or virtual organisations, one of the key distinguishing characteristics of these emerging organisations is their ultra-slim centres. Like most organisations, having divested themselves of non-core activities, they buy-in services and facilities from the marketplace under a series of subcontracting arrangements, but their outstanding characteristic is the comprehensiveness with which this is achieved. This can be illustrated by a Silicon Valley company, germanely and boldly enough called First Virtual Company. First Virtual was founded in 1993 by Ralph Ungermann, a Silicon Valley veteran. The company specialises in 'intelligent' hardware.

What makes First Virtual unusual is more what it does not do than what it does, for its 35 employees include no finance staff, no personnel representatives, no manufacturing people, no PR, no lawyers, and no international staff. It is a small company which has taken outsourcing – usually a tactic confined to the big players – to heart. Ungermann's view is that the company has two core competencies: developing engineering solutions and signing deals with powerful marketing partners around the world. Thus, all else the company may do is outsourced. First Virtual lives up to its name: it only does core – dangerously anorexic you might suppose – but clearly the company has a sufficiently developed *raison d'être*, sufficient financial resources and a sufficiently viable product to sustain itself in business. Here the equilibrium between operating economy and contracting efficiency has been with virtually all the company's activities out-sourced. Perhaps because of this extreme arrangement, company policy dictates that the staff share an open plan office in Santa Clara: a configuration designed to limit both internal misunderstandings and unnecessary demarcations. A company like First Virtual symbolically enough, exists, and perhaps can only exist, in an economic 'hot-spot', that is, in a milieu where entrepreneurial risk, flexibility and business acumen are a valued dimension of the region's economic DNA. Here 'smart' offices complete with nameplates and receptionists are available at a day's notice, venture capitalists actively and relentlessly scout for talent and commercial lawyers take their fees in equity, not cash.

One of the key core functions of the virtual organisation is, by definition, the negotiation, contracting and managing of outsourced functions and capabilities. In a traditional organisation these outsourced arrangements are semi-permanent and the function so contracted continuously required by the 'mother' organisation. However, in a virtual organisation, these functions are provided only when required, and may thus be discontinuously supplied. At one point the 'organisation' may consist of a team of 6,000 people, at another of 300, and the teams may be either highly concentrated physically or, more probably, highly dispersed geographically. Such virtual organisations share a second and equally key distinguishing feature and that is their reliance on sophisticated, networked communications. This brings added flexibility to the core team.

Thus, depending on the degree of divestiture and the degree of connectivity, such virtual organisations become loosely connected webs of agents and brokers, with a central core of staff setting a strategic direction and providing the operational support necessary to sustain the network. Such structures are therefore highly flexible with a wide tolerance towards environmental uncertainty as they have few commitments to either production capital or non-core personnel.

Christopher Barnatt describes it thus in his book *Cyberbusiness*:

> With the emergence of networked organisational forms drawing together different parties into discrete contracts, licensing agreements and joint ventures as required, distinguishing the boundaries of organisations in terms of discrete physical infrastructures, and the legal perimeters of their individual component players, clearly no longer provides a valid means of organisational analysis.[71]

As Barnatt notes it is only when a range of specialists are brought together, in a manner similar to that required for, say, the production of a feature film or a theatrical performance, that an organisation in the more traditional sense can be seen to be in operation. Dynamic network arrangements are therefore entities to be delineated by contractual agreements between their discrete players, rather than by physical offices, production plants and a host of employees which belong to the more traditional, enduring, hierarchical and structured organisations of the past.

LIMITS TO VIRTUALITY

There must, however, be limits to this reductionist process, to this virtualising act – or are we really saying that most of us will be scattered across the virtual landscape, equipped only with our mobile connectivity and without an office or factory to call our own? Where does 'unbundling' become 'unravelling'? When does casting off the burden of size, and of physical assets, hierarchies, layers and technological incompatibilities, become a nightmare of disassociated enterprises, uneasy partnerships, unfocused activity and disparate ambitions?

Logic dictates that this rationalisation process must stop somewhere – but where? If this was a tricky question in the early 1990s, it is almost certainly a much trickier question at the end of the decade. As we have seen, the boundaries to a business used to be tangible, discrete and identifiable and, indeed, encompassed the whole value chain, but not so any more. Superimposed on the delayering, outsourcing, downsizing and rationalisations of the late 1980s and early 1990s has been the recent disintermediation phenomenon triggered by the Internet. All this de-constructing has led to a rather fundamental question over what actually constitutes the core of the business. What is essential and what is non-essential to the integrity of the business? What are the quintessential features of a business which, if removed, annul the business? We must ask ourselves why we should employ anyone other than the project managers if it is possible, and indeed desirable, to outsource all stages in the value chain. If the only essential characteristics of a business are its customer relations and its branding, plus being smart enough to manage the network of contractual relations demanded of such a sliver of a corporation, then why define the organisation beyond these functions? Why indeed?

Is Virtuality Really Virtuous?

Henry Chesbrough and David Teece raise this very question in their article, 'When is Virtual Virtuous?'[72] They maintain that there are clear circumstances when being virtual is not virtuous. In fact there are circumstances when it proves highly detrimental to be so organised.

In order to discern whether virtuality or high fidelity should be the guiding light of organisational form, we first have to jettison some of our prejudices. We have come to believe unreservedly, or so it seems, that firm structure is bad and virtuality is good. Most of us would agree that excessive rigidity, hierarchy, bureaucracy and stasis are inappropriate to highly competitive business life in the late 1990s. However, flexibility and adaptability are not necessarily the undisputed gods of good. They can lead to ambiguity, dissipation and aggregated uncertainty. They can camouflage confusion and subterfuge. In trying to be too flexible and too adaptable we may lose precision, direction and drive. If we're too tenuously connected, we may lack spine and cohesion. What is needed is balance: structure and flex, grip and give, flux and flow.

The balance will fall in different places, at different times, in different businesses. We will cut the mustard in different ways. One of Chesbrough and Teece's central theses is that large integrated companies, willing to invest heavily in what is proprietary knowledge and competitive advantage, are the most appropriate organisational forms for 'systemic' innovation. They distinguish between systemic and autonomous innovation, maintaining that the latter, but not the former, may indeed be achieved very effectively by a virtual organisation. One of the critical issues is ownership, for ownership, in part at least, determines control and an ability to nurture capability. Without control there can be no effective direction.

While ownership, control and strategic leverage are the hallmarks of large corporations, incentives and responsiveness, as Chesbrough and Teece term it, are the characteristics of virtual companies. They specialise in attracting the very best talent for a specific project, typically by offering attractive bonuses, stock options and other comparable perks. This works as long as the company has the financial wherewithal to offer the highest rates. It is a highly advantageous arrangement where technology is changing rapidly and thus where different skillsets are required in rapid succession. However, as the competitive temperature rises, the cost of attracting this talent rises, as does the possibility of that same talent migrating to a competitor company. Moreover, as incentives become greater and risk-taking increases, cohesion amongst all the parties becomes more difficult to sustain, precisely because so much personal reward is at stake. Each subcontracted, associate or alliance partner necessarily acts in his or her own self-interest.

It is indeed true that smaller 'networked' competitors can outperform many larger, more cumbersome organisations. Their smallness and their connectivity, and thus the absence of decision-making layers and delaying corporate structures, means that they can act to undermine the competition – providing of course that they have the financial resources, the market capability, the competitive 'clout' and the negotiating power to do so. Here we come close to the rub. This is not to say that these advantages are necessarily absent from a virtual organisation: far from it. However, if corporate presence is ethereally dispersed or financial wherewithal diluted in any way – or if it even appears so to the financiers, the analysts, the journalists, your competitors, or indeed your potential allies – then the virtual organisation is a less powerful competitor than the integrated corporate giant. As a rule of thumb, the greater the amount of decentralisation, the more dilute the strategic leverage.

Supposing we take virtuality to its logical conclusion and assume that a virtual company's only real investment is in its project managers and contract lawyers. Important though these people are, both corporately and individually, this is hardly a sufficient base on which to grow a business. In order to reap, a company has to sow. In business, rewards come through substantial and continual investment in research, development, prototyping, application production and wide dissemination on the international market. If twenty companies have formed an alliance to bring a product to market, then the spoils of market success must be split in twenty different ways. While risk has been minimised, so, necessarily, has individual gain. So, we ask ourselves, is it really possible to invest in a minuscule way and yet be a major force on the world scene? Probably not. Whether we are talking about business success or personal achievements, greatness usually necessitates considerable and sustained investment.

In the case of a cumbersome organisation, further re-sculpting and paring would yield an altogether more robust and competitive entity, but there are limits to reductionism and virtualisation beyond which the organisation loses its competitive leverage, its negotiating power, its market presence and its 'sense of self'. The key question in business has become one of finding the right size for the organisation – rightsizing rather than downsizing. As Eric Almquist, a vice president at New York-based Mercer Management Consulting Inc., has said: 'Nobody shrinks to greatness.'

The Twin Liabilities

While a virtual organisation has many attractive characteristics, including its adaptability, its fleetness of foot, its microlight overheads and its energy, this form of organisation does have some downsides. Whether we are talking about a large corporation with largely isolated employees scattered across the globe, or about a loose alliance of contractors, partners and associates, either way too disparate a formation leaves the virtual corporation vulnerable.

There are two major forms of liability which a virtual organisation must face. The first is the risk of dwindling motivation and low morale. This is a particular hazard for teleworkers or telecommuters – employees working from home and thus isolated and physically remote from the 'mother ship', give or take a telecommunication link back to base. This arrangement may, in certain circumstances, work exceedingly well and operate to promote efficient self-management. It may however contribute to disorientation, lack of stimulus, a fading sense of 'belonging' and a yearning for office camaraderie. There is a danger that employees become office 'nomads', operating from a series of diffused satellite offices and only touching the corporate office on occasion. The computer company, IBM, for example, has fixed desk space for only one in two of its workers and plans, in the future, to provide 'permanent' office accommodation for only 20 per cent of its workforce; the assumption being that, at any given moment, 80 per cent of the workforce will be out on the cyberspace road.

Where transient and *ad hoc* team working is the norm, the corporate office environment may become so transient that the very concept of office accommodation loses its meaning. So called 'hot-desk environments' and 'hotelling arrangements' are symptomatic of this trend. 'Hot-desking' abandons the notion of having individual desks for individual employees. Instead, many communal desks or 'consoles' are provided with networked computing facilities. Thus, irrespective of which console you pull down for use (they tend to ride up and down from the ceiling) – whether you're in Tobago, Toronto or Totnes – you can access your own files and the required corporate data. Effectively, the facilities of a mobile laptop have been seamlessly combined with intranet access and embodied in a surreal office. Taking the first step to nomadism, companies like Anderson Consulting, Chiat/Day and Howell Henry Chaldecott Lury have introduced this form of vagabond existence.

Closely related to the hot-desk development is the hotelling arrangement: the latter perhaps a slightly upmarket version of the former. Here the company has employed a 'concierge' whose task it is to arrange corporate office facilities for employees in advance of their arrival. A temporary office or office 'cubicle' is then provided for the duration of the executive's visit, on which their nameplate will have been displayed in advance. Clearly this arrangement makes a great deal of corporate sense where the organisation is internationally based and where employees, by the nature of their employment, are rarely in the office. Like hot-desk arrangements, the hotelling concept relies on organisation-wide communications networks, and high specification computer hardware through which all work is directed.

These arrangements have clear benefits to a competitive company. Not least, they enable a company to move forward, transfer energy and re-focus very quickly in response to, or in anticipation of, market changes. However, these arrangements also have costs. Being so reliant on networked electronic communications, virtuality breeds a new form of technological dependence and, being so improvised, it also breeds a new source of social vulnerability. Referring to the American historian, Christopher Lasch, the *Guardian* journalist, Larry Elliott notes: '[He] is in no doubt that the appetite for a world of change, movement and uncertainty is confined to the new peripatetic elite . . .' He quotes Lasch: 'Advancement in business and the professions, these days, requires a willingness to follow the siren call of opportunity wherever it leads. Those who stay at home forfeit the chance of upward mobility. Ambitious people understand, then, that a migratory way of life is the price of getting ahead.'[73]

Larry Elliott also notes in the same article, but in a wider social context: 'Culturally there is a backlash. The focus groups used to test public opinion have detected that there is a reaction against anonymity and alienation . . .' Clearly this is a corporate danger which besets telecommuting, hot-desking and hotelling, particularly if it is compounded with short-term contracts, pronounced discontinuity, lack of leadership and a failure to compensate for remoteness and transience. If discontinuity grows into drift and disorientation, then sooner or later both the company and the individual lose out. Cyberspace is no home to live in. As the American sociologist, Richard Sennet, has observed, an overall gain in flexibility may equate with an existential loss of security.[74]

The second form of liability to which a virtual organisation is susceptible is one of conflicting interests. This turns on the issue of control, coherence, loyalty and integrity. If, instead of having a large body of 'virtual' employees (as in large numbers of telecommuters or hot-desk employees), the virtual organisation consists of a series of corporate alliances, then the issue of how to avoid conflicting interests and split loyalties becomes paramount. Moreover as in a cumbersome, but integrated organisation, the greater the number of separate negotiations and consultations required before action is effected, the more flat-footed and clumsy an organisation becomes. In alliances and joint ventures there is also the issue of the equality of the parties, for inevitably there will be differentials or inequalities in capability. The skill of the alliance managers is to ensure mutuality triumphs over any attempts at subversion, however inadvertent, by the dominant partner/s. The moment inequalities create undue and intended advantage, the power of mutuality is compromised and the coherence of the alliance endangered.

Another key skill in sustaining an alliance or a joint venture is knowing what information is proprietary to any one of the parties to the alliance, and what constitutes the common pool of knowledge from which the alliance can draw. What intellectual assets are regarded as legitimately common to the alliance? For employees whose loyalty is exclusively dedicated to one organisation, the issue of allegiance is rarely complicated or under threat of compromise; however, for alliance partners and associates, recognition of proprietary knowledge and, if shared, acknowledgement of its confidentiality is one of the key issues of business ethics.

The issue is fairly cut and dried if the performance of the alliance depends on information already captured – for example, already codified and documented in technical standards, component specifications or promotional campaign strategies. However, since much advantage in business is derived from the application of intuitive understanding and accumulated nous, the more challenging question is to what extent these intellectual assets should be shared. The answer turns, at least in part, on how critical this knowledge is to the core business of any one of the alliance signatories. The moment that knowledge becomes 'core critical' to any one of the partners, the joint venture will begin to falter. Virtuality, then, has its strengths, but evidently it also has its weaknesses.

GLOBAL CONNECTIVITY

Whichever dimension of virtuality you hone in on, you can be sure that it will be underpinned by corporate or alliance-based connectivity – and connectivity on a global basis. Competition has made this necessary and technology has made it possible.

In the last 150 years technological advances have increased mobility to such an extent that it is now unremarkable for someone to have travelled the globe extensively. Indeed, in business terms, this is regarded as normal. In the last fifteen years advances in computer mobility have been superimposed on those of physical mobility, opening up the possibility of global connectivity. The ability to deliver computing power, regardless of whether the point of delivery is a laptop (unfixed) or a desktop (fixed), relies on a number of technologies including portable hardware, global networks – principally the Internet – and wireless data communications. It is precisely the convergence of those technologies that finally allows the computer to be truly mobile. Moreover, as the price premium for portability shrinks and the technology gap between portables and desktop machines narrows, the likelihood that portables will replace desktops increases. By way of proof, portable PC manufacturers, like Toshiba, Compaq, IBM and Dell are making noticeable inroads into the desktop market, offering high-end notebook machines with fast Pentium MMX microprocessors and high-speed integrated CD-ROM drives. In 1997, about one in every three PCs sold in the USA and one in every five in Europe was a mobile machine.[75]

The IT consultancy firm, Gartner Group, estimates that by the year 2000, 55 million laptop computer users will work outside the boundaries of the enterprise. Moreover, they will do so without the benefit of local area networks or high-speed wide area network connections (that is, proprietary systems) at least 20 per cent of the time.[76] These users include telecommuters, 'migratory' or 'vagabond' workers and truly mobile workers, for example, field service technicians. Not far beyond the year 2000 more than 75 per cent of 'knowledge workers' will be 'location-independent' predicts Gartner.

Reflecting this trend, portable PC sales are expected to more than double from $30 billion to nearly $80 billion by the end of the decade, an 18 per cent compound annual growth rate, according to a recent study of pen, palmtop and notebook computers prepared by Frost and Sullivan, the market research company. This demand is driven, at least in part, by companies replacing desktops with portable PCs which are sold with PC card network devices, docking stations or port replicators, enabling them to integrate easily with corporate networks. Meanwhile, the development of the portable PC as a communications device has meant that notebook PCs can have high-speed remote access to e-mail, the Internet and to corporate intranets anytime and anywhere. Consequentially, mobile capability is seen less and less as a separate entity and more and more as an extension of the corporate IT infrastructure, and thus of the company's knowledge base.

Another element in the virtual armoury of the corporate executive is the mobile phone, although what was a clear distinction between mobile computing and mobile phoning is now beginning to fade. Mobile phones, and thus digital wireless communications generally, have traditionally suffered some communication disadvantages. Key among them has been low bandwidth which has limited the amount of data that can be sent, and the speed with which it can be transmitted. The Global System for Mobile (GSM) wireless network – now a standard across Europe – allows only 9,600 bits per second (bps) compared with 28,800 bps or higher through a standard phone landline. For the moment, the integration of computer and net based capability has to be developed within those limitations.

However, progress is being made. For example, the Finnish company Nokia launched its 9600 product in 1996, bringing e-mail messaging to a mobile phone (as demonstrated by Val Kilmer in the 1997 film, *The Saint*). Basically the 9600 is a hand-held phone with a built-in screen and keyboard so you can access e-mail, fax messages and the Internet through a GSM network. Telecoms company Nortel plans to take this concept further in early 1998 with the launch of telephones that run Java software and incorporate a stylus to write or draw directly on to the screen for e-mail or fax transmission. The product – code-named Ovbitor – was demonstrated at the 1997 BT Innovations exhibition and will be launched in collaboration with specific network service providers.

Connectivity Exemplified

The following series of product launches, reported during the period winter 1996 to summer 1997, illustrate how developments in global connectivity are unfolding. The first two – the Mobiq and BT Pacific – relate to satellite communications; the third relates to Netscape's intranet policy; the fourth to multi-function smart cards; and the fifth and sixth to 'hardwear' (wearable hardware) and wristwatch telephony respectively. Collectively they paint a picture of how the digital landscape will build, and thus they help us to get a concrete fix on the future lest it become all too 'virtual'.

Mobiq

A satellite phone no bigger or heavier than a notebook PC has been developed and launched in a joint initiative by BT and Norway's Telnor, who claim that it is the world's smallest global mobile communications system. Called the Mobiq and weighing just 2.2 kilos, it can be used, say the makers, from virtually any land mass, even from the Himalayas where previously cellular phones have been ineffective. While sacrificing sound quality for portability and economy, the Mobiq performed well when used by Sandy Gall, the writer and broadcaster, while leading an expedition across the Omani Desert.[77]

The high power of new generation satellites, like the Inmarsat satellites positioned over the equator which provides links for the Mobiq, means that less power is needed on the ground. This paves the way for smaller terminals and cheaper call charges. Users dial an international number as they would if they were using a conventional landline phone. The Mobiq delivers digitised voice, fax and data communications, including e-mail and comes as a complete package of telephone and air time. It is operated with a removable SIM card which offers security and allows users to share telephones while retaining their billing data and storing speed dial numbers on their personal cards.

BT Pacific

When the new £15 million Land Earth Station in Auckland went live in the summer of 1997, BT offered its customers a service that, apart from the polar regions, will span the whole world. Called BT Pacific, the station will work in tandem with BT's existing land earth stations, BT Atlantic (formerly Goonhilly) in the UK and BT Indian at Eik in Norway.[78]

The station provides the earth link for the Inmarsat Pacific Ocean region satellite and offers a full range of communications facilities including voice, fax, telex, data and high-speed data capabilities. It also plans to introduce applications such as video conferencing, Internet access and e-mail. BT's New Zealand partner, telecommunications provider Clear, has assisted by providing the national and international links to the BT global voice and data networks. BT's communications systems for maritime and land mobile use including Inmarsat-A, B-Sat, M-Sat, C-Sat and Mobiq.

Netscape's Intranet Policy

After a year locked in combat with Microsoft to win the 'browser wars', Netscape announced in October 1996 that it intended to concentrate on intranets, the internal corporate networks which are widely seen as more lucrative. Jim Barksdale, president and chief executive of Netscape told satellite-linked audiences in California, New York and London that the proposals marked the beginning of a 'third wave' of the Net. 'Our goal,' he said, 'is to obtain a 75 per cent share of the $10 billion market for corporate intranets over the next five years, building on the success of the Netscape name.'[79]

The main announcement covered two new suites of Net software designed to bring workgroup functionality to Web-based intranets. The company released details of a new version of its Web Server system, SuiteSpot 3.0, which provides tools for a network administrator to build and maintain a company intranet. With the market for intranets using Internet technology within a company or private network set to grow, Netscape will position SuiteSpot to compete with Lotus, Novell, IBM and Microsoft for a share of the intranet spoils.

Netscape also announced the Netscape Communication suite which includes version 4.0 of the company's Navigator Web browser as well as modules that will provide secure e-mail, groupware (thus challenging established vendors like IBM/Lotus with its Notes products and Novell with GroupWise) and collaboration features. From November 1996, Navigator became part of a suite of software called Netscape Communicator, which also includes: Messenger, an application that allows Web content to be sent as e-mail; Collabra, a reader that can search across Internet discussion groups and local network-based groups at the same time; Composer, an editing tool for creating Web documents and e-mail; and Conference, which lets users talk to each other, share documents, transfer files and dial Internet phone numbers. Rolled into the software is a conference component and a program to schedule meetings using a centralised calendar.

In a surprising move, the company announced that future Netscape products would integrate more fully with Microsoft

Office and other Microsoft products such as Windows 95 and SQL Server. The reason for providing this 'embrace and integrate' strategy, according to Marc Andreesen, co-founder of the company, was to ensure the corporate customer could mix and match products to get the best fit for their organisation.

Multi-Function Smart Cards

IBM presented its vision of the future of air travel – ticketless travel and smart cards – at the IATA Passenger Services Conference in Los Angeles in October 1996.[80] Linked to this vision was IBM's announcement, in association with American Express, of a new multi-function smart card.

The technology, developed by IBM, lets you book an airline ticket at a travel agent, at the airport or over the Internet without having to be served by staff. Using a touchscreen booth, travellers can select preferred flights from various menu options and insert the combined smart card and American Express card to pay for the flight and download details of the flight into the card's memory.

Upon arrival at the airport, the traveller inserts the card in a reader to check in, choosing a preferred seat and other variables at the same time. The smart card can then be used as the boarding pass. At no time during this process is a ticket issued to the traveller. The smart card not only contains the flight information and other details about the journey, but can also store other information about the passenger, acting as an ID card to confirm the travel arrangements and containing personal information.

Hardwear

Promoted as the gadget that no well-dressed business executive should be without, the Office-on-the-Arm is a wearable integrated PC, electronic organiser and video communicator. Seen as the start of 'body furniture', thanks to the convergence of computing, telecommunications and electronics, it has been developed into a fully working prototype by BT research laboratories.[81]

The wearable office system is based on an Apple Macintosh palmtop and includes a colour screen, a touchpad for direct input similar to a mouse and a microphone for voice recognition. By use of digital mobile phone links, it can also communicate directly with other computers – back at the office or with other colleagues – so that the wearer can access the Internet, fax and e-mail messages.

One of the principal limitations at the moment is that the system is limited by battery life (four hours), but BT hopes the future version will be powered by heat from the wearer's body.

Wristwatch Telephony

The Japanese telecommunications giant, NTT, has developed a wristwatch telephone which it plans to bring to market in 1998.[82] One of the key challenges in shrinking a mobile phone to the size of a watch is in fabricating a sufficiently small, and a sufficiently powerful, power supply and receiver. NTT has achieved this by removing most of the hardware associated with a mobile phone and locating it into a base station that is connected to the national phone network. The watch-phone sends all its communications via radio link to the base station. The watch itself has only four buttons for the primary functions, such as switching on and off and checking battery levels, with everything else functioning distantly from the base station.

To dial, the owner speaks the numbers into the microphone or repeats the name of someone whose number has been recorded. The request is sent by the radio link to the nearest base station where speech-recognition software converts it into the correct dialling pulses which are then sent down the national phone network. When the call is connected the base station immediately relays the answer to a small loudspeaker on the watch-phone, or to an earphone if preferred. In prototype, the watch-phone weighs 70 grams, including the battery. NTT is working to reduce the weight before planning to put the new design on sale before the end of 1997.

VIRTUAL COLLABORATION

One of the key business implications for such global connectivity is the ability it gives colleagues to collaborate internationally in real-time despite being scattered across varying time zones and latitudes. It also provides the ability to spin off erstwhile physical production activities into an ethereal, virtual space. In any manufacturing process, for example, it is increasingly likely that product design, prototyping and product testing functions will migrate to the virtual world in addition to the R&D function. This will be the case particularly where the intellectual input into the manufactured item is high and/or production cost is high. In cyberspace, proposals, design documents, prototype specifications and business plans, for example, can be exchanged internationally at the touch of a button, and computerised simulations can test different design possibilities with endless ease at near-zero incremental cost per synthetic prototype. That ability reduces the financial risks which would otherwise be encountered at the design stage. Also, because the product development stage can be progressed faster in cyberspace than in the physical world, companies deploying this technology gain in two ways: not only do they steal a march on their competitors, but they also enjoy shorter return on investment cycles.

Spaced Out

The following series of business activities reported in 1997 shows how digital connectivity and virtual reality are progressively being embedded in the processes and functions of business. Working practices at the Hothouse Centre, at Ford Motors, and at ADTranz illustrate the incorporation of virtual reality and computer simulation techniques in the design and prototype stages of manufacture; the production process adopted for the animation film, *Space Jam*, illustrates the collaborative power of global connectivity; and the extranet systems developed by FedEx and Cisco Systems illustrate the economy and competitive edge which can be derived from facilitating electronic customer access to erstwhile exclusively internal company databases.

The Hothouse centre for ceramic design lies inside the Gladstone Pottery Museum in Longton, Stoke-on-Trent, an area dominated by the pottery industry. It offers manufacturers and designers access to hi-tech design and modelling tools with Unix workstations, PCs and Apple Macs available and technical support on hand; a facility particularly valuable to small businesses. It also runs a post-graduate training scheme and recruits young designers, training them to use CAD/CAM (computer-aided design/manufacturing) systems, and imparts skills involved in establishing a design business.[83]

Contemporary design software allows potters to take a concept right through the production process – for example producing 3-D objects on screen, outputting this directly as a photographic image to be featured in a product catalogue, and feeding production specifications directly into a computer-controlled milling machine where a prototype can be produced. Available software includes the DeskArtes shape design program which was originally used for Saab cars. Now standard in ceramics, it is a virtualisation tool with good surface data that can reproduce a glazed appearance or the reflectivity of porcelain. Platescribe software was developed by a British company, Typemaker, for the ceramics industry in conjunction with Royal Doulton. It uses Apple Macs to create design units in Adobe Illustrator and Photoshop so that they can be repeated and bent to fit any specified path. Another program, PS-Virtualiser, can map the newly created designs directly on to a scanned photograph of 3-D whiteware, eliminating the need to create complicated 3-D models of existing shapes.

Together this suite of software eliminates much of the hard graft of design and prototype production for client consideration in the ceramics business, and compresses the pre-production cycle into a shorter time. Similar software means, for example, that the ceramics company, Spode, can launch a range of tableware in nine months instead of what would otherwise have taken three years. Moreover, Stoke's big names, like Royal Doulton and Wedgwood, now have ISDN links between the design studios in Stoke and their New York Offices. This way prototype images can be transmitted electronically for preview and consideration by American clients and video discussions concerning the designs are held in real time between the American clients and the British designers.

Meanwhile, train builders ADTranz of Derby have deployed a virtual reality system from the Bristol-based company Division to allow it to prototype its new fleet of Electrostar trains.[84] Although these trains will not be operational until 1999, they have been, as it were, virtually operational in cyberspace since spring 1997. Virtual reality has allowed engineers to step forward in time to create the new trains in full working detail without the need for expensive physical mock-ups and prototypes. They run on virtual tracks and stop at cyberstations where the virtual doors open. Incorporating the ability to simulate the cumulative effect of wear and tear means that potential design weaknesses can be highlighted, subsequently modified and guidelines given on recommended maintenance routines. This way the most cost-effective performance can be attained over the entire 20-year operating lifespan of the trains.

The Ford Motor Company has taken similar steps into the

virtual world. Over the last decade it has invested significantly in computer-aided design and manufacturing systems, groupware and video conferencing facilities. It employed these technology tools very effectively, for example, in the development of its 'global car', marketed in North America as the Cantour sedan. Rather than creating national product teams or convening elaborate design summits, the company established an internationally-dispersed virtual design team. Not only did this arrangement negate the need for costly executive travel, it gave Ford access to the best engineering, design and marketing talent worldwide.

Ford is now planning to take the concept of virtual connectivity further down the value chain and into the assembly process itself. It has been one of the first car manufacturers to explore using computer simulations to design its vehicle final assembly processes on a global basis. If the concept goes into general use, it will slice an estimated £1.5 billion off carmakers' costs.[85] In the past, product design engineers would design a component, a (physical) prototype part would be made and then manufacturing engineers and product specialists would work to make the assembly process feasible. It is now planned that manufacturing engineers and product design engineers will work alongside one another, using the same computer images of vehicle components and facilities. Assembly techniques would then be developed at the same time as components are designed, thereby reducing the company's reliance on expensive prototypes early in the product development process and shortening the critical time to market. Ford plans to use its new digital system, C3P – an integrated computer-aided design, engineering, manufacturing and product information management system – in the development of all its critical manufacturing processes from the year 2000.

Film-making is another example of a production process which has been intimately affected by digitisation. Most visibly, it has facilitated the deployment of exotic cinematographic techniques and the design of spectacular special effects as witnessed, for example, in the title sequence of *GoldenEye* or in the films *The Fifth Element*, *Toy Story*, *Men in Black* and *Jumanji*. It has also enabled collaborative teamwork on a global basis. Warner Brothers' film, *Space Jam*, which opened in Britain in March 1997, incorporates a mix of live action, traditional hand-drawn animation and computer-generated animation. Its production relied upon a sophisticated network of digital connectivity between ten different studios, six in America and four in London.

As the film's Hollywood director needed to check each frame of animation at several different stages of development, fast transmission of the files, and thus a high-speed computer network, was essential. *Space Jam* used a combination of multiple ISDN telephone lines and a large-capacity data line across the Atlantic to allow Hollywood and London animators to work on the film simultaneously.[86] Each frame took up about 45 megabytes of digital space, with each finished two to three second shot taking up to six to ten gigabytes. During the production process, line drawings were also exchanged each day, scanned by Cinesite and transmitted to Warner Brothers' Hollywood office where a computer named 'Jammer' coordinated the huge amount of data. Jammer enabled all the studios involved to see exactly what frames of animation and live action were available, and to retrieve the appropriate footage when required. Live-action film was scanned in using one of the few laser film scanners which are currently operational.

According to Uli Meyer, one of the animation directors on the film, whose London animation studio contributed around a third of the film's sequences, the nightly video-conferencing sessions were critical to success. He also believes the film has helped stop the 'brain drain' of animators to Hollywood because the technology enabled the 'creatives' to remain at their home bases on different sides of the Atlantic. It also enabled the film to be made in a short space of time, which was necessary since Michael Jordan – the American basketball player, a key character in the film – was only available for a three-month slot. The film was completed in about nine months, a process which, without the technology, would normally have taken around two years.

Another dimension is the digitising of a company's external links in the creation of a web of connectivity amongst itself, its suppliers, its customers and its partners. Federal Express and Cisco Systems provide good examples. They identify three levels of information access: internal release only (intranets); controlled inter-company release (extranets); and no-holds-barred public release (the Internet).

Both companies have taken a strategic decision to create extranets by opening their internal database systems to direct electronic access by customers, clients and partners. Not only does this give their suppliers and clients direct access to information, from anywhere in the world at any time, about ordered products, it also effectively blurs the boundaries between the company and its partners. Through their intranet and extranet developments, both companies show how digital connectivity is dissolving the discrete physical infrastructures which previously, and effectively, demarcated a company's operating parameters.

Federal Express (FedEx) is an international company, with headquarters in Memphis, USA. It specialises in package transportation worldwide. Over the last twenty-four months or so, it has extended its Internet presence by encouraging its clients to tap directly, and electronically, into its package database. Thus the FedEx Internet site now offers its customers three specific features. First, it tracks the location and status of their package, from anywhere in the world to anywhere in the world, at any point en-route. Second, it provides the means to prepare the shipping paperwork from the corporate Web site with a mandatory fill-in screen prompt (primary delays are due to incomplete shipping paperwork). Third, its individual country sites offer information on international package shipping rules and regulations and related documentation. As of June 1997, FedEx had over 500,000 digitally 'connected' customers worldwide. Over 65 per cent of its 2.7 million packages transported daily were transported to net-connected customers. FedEx's corporate strategy is to move all communication with clients about their package transportation to an online environment.

In terms of site traffic, FedEx receives 3.2 million 'hits' a month from 117 different countries; 1.04 million packages are tracked by customers every month; and 45,000 packages are shipped per month in the USA. Not only has FedEx's extranet provided an enhanced service to customers, it has led to significant corporate savings. The company estimates that over 50 per cent of its customers now tracking their packages on the Net would have called FedEx's customer services phone line had the extranet not existed. This means that FedEx has to deal with over 50 per cent fewer calls, so, given that the company would otherwise receive about 1.04 million phone calls a month, FedEx has reduced the pressure on its phone answering service by over 500,000 phone calls a month.[87] These savings amply compensate for the cost of building and maintaining the site.

From FedEx's perspective the success factors in this extranet, or corporate-client net, development include the following: (a) it constitutes a natural extension to its existing service – customers already understood the nature of FedEx business which is now being enhanced or re-constructed by the extranet; (b) the development leverages existing systems as FedEx already shares information with its customers; (c) the seamless and global nature of the medium makes it easily comprehensive and unitary; (d) the transaction-based rather than static nature of the information; (e) the fact that technological expertise is a core competency of FedEx and thus the extranet strategy compatible with its core strategy; and, (f) that the strong collaboration between FedEx's internal IT and marketing teams has made the extranet a success.

Cisco Systems has effected a similar sort of development. Cisco is one of the leading companies worldwide in the assembly and supply of networked hardware systems. As IT is its core business, it would undoubtedly endorse the words of Glover Ferguson of Andersen Consulting: 'how companies use information technology will define their success in the coming era of virtual business'. Cisco has effectively become a borderless company in that its globally-based employees, customers, partners and suppliers now all share the enterprise's information database. Moreover, by the nature of the products Cisco sells, it enables other companies to achieve the same networked status.

Cisco Systems identifies the business drivers to networking as profitability and productivity, competitive advantage, and organisational structure – finding the right corporate size. By adopting a networked model for its own company, and encouraging direct supplier and customer interrogation of its corporate databases, thus cutting out all corporate intermediaries, Cisco estimates that it saves over $383 million a year. This consists of $125 million in support (via corporate 'disintermediation'); $8.4 million in hiring (through electronic advertising and support); $85 million on software; and $165 million on paper-related transactions (now electronically executed). This is on a business costing $1.8 billion to run, so about 20 per cent has been shaved off its annual corporate costs. Approximately 13 per cent of all Cisco business was generated through business-to-business networked commerce in early 1997, and doubtless this will rise significantly over the next five years.

The Migration to Nets

The Internet has, unwittingly as it were, not only changed the rules of the game, but also its nature. In the process, the information technology (IT) function within an organisation has changed from a tactical corporate accoutrement to a strategic backbone, for now, technology enables a company to automate its existing business practices and, critically, provides it with the capability to re-invent its business. The convergence of computers and telecommunications has begun, very effectively, to blur the distinctions between and amongst the Internet, intranets and extranets, and in the process camouflages the company's physical boundaries. Thus the 'factory gate' is no longer a fixed physical entity; it is a fluid electronic parameter.

So pervasive will computer networking become that companies which retain customer- and supplier-related information on a proprietary 'legacy' system will effectively be shooting themselves in the foot. They will be overtaken competitively by companies which have slicker communication systems and much reduced overheads. The extent to which Internet-based systems are overtaking proprietary systems can be illustrated by reference to GE Information Services (GEIS) and the services this company offers to the marketplace.

GEIS, the electronic transactional processing group based in Rockville, Maryland, made its reputation providing reliable, heavy-duty data links and proprietary electronic data interchange (EDI) services for its corporate customers. However, when the Internet began to be adopted by corporate users for communications and electronic commerce, many people questioned whether GEIS could adapt to the fast-paced environment. Some even asked whether electronic data interchange itself had a future.

Harry Seegers, CEO of GEIS, has been quoted as saying that information technology will be to the twenty-first century what electricity has been to the twentieth: 'It [IT] will transform the nature of business and be a leading contributor to economic productivity. We must position our business as the world leader in business applications of information technology for the next century.'[88] He believes IT will enable companies to 'streamline their supply chain processes, achieve quantum improvements in product quality, dramatically expand their market reach, and tightly integrate operations with those of trading partners'.

Recognising the critical role of the Internet, and thus global connectivity more generally, GEIS is changing the emphasis in its business. In the services it offers it now seeks to combine the advantages of secure, high quality private networks with the ease of use and lower cost attributes of Internet technologies. It seeks to apply its understanding of horizontal communications. Thus, GEIS believes that, rather than posing a threat to EDI-based systems, open Internet technologies will enhance their reach. The company has, for example, pioneered the use of EDI over the Internet with TradeWeb, an entry-level, forms-based service which enables subscribers to send and receive four basic EDI documents – the purchase order, purchase order acknowledgement, invoice and functional acknowledgement – over the Internet using a standard Web browser. It has also developed sales force automation and logistics tracking services as part of the specific intranet and extranet applications it is offering its customers.

As noted in Durlacher's *Intranet Report 1997*, within the next few years intranet technologies will become the primary way in which corporate legacy systems are accessed.[89] This will give rise to a vibrant market in products which link the old and the new. Executives at GEIS believe this is one way they can offer added value – by working closely with the open systems providers and helping them to derive maximum value from their applications through interconnectivity with legacy systems. However, Harry Seegers believes that private networks will endure. Quoting from experience, he says, 'Chief executives and chief information officers tell me that the day they do mission-critical transactions on the public networks is the day pigs will fly.' Clearly, and rightly, companies will hug information which is critical to their core operations close to their corporate breasts.

Price Waterhouse, in its 1998 *Technology Forecast* study, echoes similar sentiments.[90] It notes how the Internet is a metaphor for future communication structures, and documents how satellite networks, telephone systems, cable and data networks are being developed to ensure that information can be accessed quickly and seamlessly. This process is likely to be accelerated in part, because the communications industry has begun to change from a traditional proprietary technology to a 'switched packet' environment in which data flows over global, interconnected networks. The convergence of computer and telecommunication technology means that the latter is now available to computer communications users with switching and routing functions seamlessly integrated.

The pervasive effect of the Internet, and the open standards which underpin it, are also apparent in the area of virtual reality (VR) where the issue of proprietary systems versus Web-based systems is currently being played out. Computer-based simulation and virtual prototyping are increasingly being used in business in the R&D phase of product development, but applications like manufacturing simulations still represent a niche market because of the high cost of the dedicated facilities required. Consequentially the VR industry is looking elsewhere for new growth. In particular, it is exploring the potential of PC-based VR systems and Web-based virtual worlds.

Training, for example, is one of the fastest-growing applications of virtual reality, and it has given many firms their first exposure to VR running on standard office PCs. PC-based systems are helping to drive down the costs of VR, but the factor that will really popularise the technology is the Web and, in particular, the Virtual Reality Modelling Language (VRML). VRML is a software standard for creating virtual worlds on Web sites. It opens up a wealth of possible applications, from virtual shopping centres to Web-based 3-D catalogues and collaborative engineering. VRML makes possible, for example, efficient transmission 3-D models over the Internet or corporate intranets and then their subsequent manipulation on screen using any VRML-compatible browser. The VR industry has for years created niche one-off solutions but VRML should bring critical mass. According to the UK market research company, Ovum, these new areas could push VR into the mainstream and create a £1 billion market by 2001, compared with just $135 million in 1995.[91]

Thus, in many ways the impact of the Internet has been profound. It has ushered in a new equality of access in business and breathtaking – bracing – possibilities for seamless connectivity. In short, it has changed the rules of the game. It has changed how companies connect, how new competitive advantage may be sought and how business relationships are developed and sustained. In turn, this has made it more difficult to define the boundaries of a company by its physical infrastructure alone. As virtuality bites home, companies and their employees or associates will have to work harder at defining their contractual obligations, and at finding a modus operandi which combines the benefits of technology with the human need for connectedness and identity. If companies – or 'enterprise envelopes' – become so shrunken that they consist only of a few virtual 'points of presence' dotted along various economic 'hot spots', then how will we recognise them? Certainly not by their factory building for this icon belonged to the Industrial Revolution and that is over. We will recognise them largely by their virtual presence. The challenge lies in combining the advantages of virtuality with the necessity for something atomistic, something 'real', and something tangible. The devil is in the balance.

Chapter 7

The Enterprise Challenge

THE ECONOMIC GOOGLY

The central event of the twentieth century is the overthrow of matter. In technology, economics, and the politics of nations, wealth in the form of physical resources is steadily declining in value and significance. The powers of the mind are everywhere ascendant over the brute force of things.[92]

So remarked technology thinker, George Gilder in his book, *Microcosm*. The observation is both true and traumatic. It means that the very nature and culture of business is undergoing transformation. Moreover, this migration to a world based on intellectual powers rather than physical powers has also led to a re-assessment of basic economic principles, as these were premised on an overwhelmingly physical world. It has also led to a re-examination of what were once regarded as irrefutable canons of economic theory. Thus, the very way in which we regard the creation of wealth and operation of the economy is undergoing a process of mutation.

In consequence this has led to something of a renaissance in economic thinking. Economists have begun to re-examine the idea, central to their discipline, that the operation of markets, and thus the business world, is determined by physical resources and the underlying tenet that such resources are limited. An economy based, at least in part, on intellectual powers, on the application of knowledge and on the propagation of ideas contravenes this basic assumption since the economics of ideas are an economics of abundance. For the sharing of ideas, far from increasing their scarcity and diminishing their value, actually enhances their economic value

164

since it increases the chances of propagation and thus the probability of innovation. Ideas and knowledge are not subject to diminishing returns nor to depreciation, but, like goodwill and brand loyalty, to increasing returns and appreciation.

The Economics of Ideas

Thus one of the hottest ideas in economics today, which is testing the minds of those at the cutting edge, is the theory of 'increasing returns'. The history of modern economic thinking since the great British economist Alfred Marshall published his seminal textbook in 1890 has been premised on the concept of 'diminishing returns' – the idea that there comes a point beyond which the investment of further capital or labour yields fewer and fewer rewards, beyond which it is economically futile to invest further. The corollary of this theory, premised on the assumption that the capital or labour invested in a business is a finite resource, is that a natural ceiling is reached in business growth, a monopolistic position averted, and a predictable equilibrium of prices and market share reached.

During the twentieth century and particularly in the last twenty years, Western economies have undergone a transformation from material manufacturing – based on the highly physical and bulky activity of oil refining, steel manufacture or grain processing, for example – to the microcosmic and essentially invisible process of transmitting information. Emphasis is moving away from the processing of physical resources to the processing of information, from the application of raw energy to the application of ideas, and from the insuring of physical assets to the safeguarding of intellectual assets. As this shift has occurred, the underlying mechanisms that determine economic behaviour have shifted from ones of diminishing returns to ones of increasing returns.

But increasing returns is not entirely new to the economic block. Economic theorists have long known about increasing returns, but prior to the 1990s, the idea did not rise to the surface of mainstream economic thinking. According to James Aley, writing in *Fortune* magazine, it tended to be shunned for both ideological and methodological reasons.[93] Ideologically, increasing returns buck the traditional system because they challenge the orthodox assumption that, other things being equal, market forces yield the best possible outcome in products and prices. They throw a further googly into the works by challenging the assumption that competition is thereby enhanced and monopolistic behaviour effectively averted. Moreover, practically speaking, increasing returns are exceedingly difficult to deal with mathematically. They muddle the mechanics of supply and demand.

However, the case for increasing returns has recently been so tightly and rigorously argued that sustaining a contrary position is becoming more difficult. One of the leading proponents of the theory is W. Brian Arthur, based at both Stanford and Santa Fe Institute, who has provided much of the mathematical rigour needed to lend the idea both credence and academic respectability. His central thesis is that in a growing number of industries, particularly those that are knowledge intensive, there is a natural tendency for the market leader to get further ahead, causing a monopolistic position to occur.

Significant contributions also come from Stanford's Paul Krugman and from Paul Romer at the University of California at Berkeley – two of the Young Turks among modern macroeconomists. Krugman's work has concentrated on how the concept of increasing returns plays out in international trade and challenges another deeply held conviction of economists: that free trade among nations always produces the best economic outcome. Taking the premise that ideas are not in themselves scarce – and with application and circulation they augment their value, unlike physical resources – Romer developed his 'new' economic growth theory in the mid 1980s. Although his work is highly theoretical and esoteric, turning on dense algebraic equations and abstract mathematics, its intellectual rigour is not in doubt, nor its central message – that new ideas, embedded in technological change, drive economic growth.

Economists such as Arthur, Krugman and Romer are not however intent on throwing the 'new economic baby' out with the 'orthodox economics bathwater'. Indeed, much of business activity is still premised on the physical world – the aviation industry, the transportation industry, service industries and construction industries – and thus is subject to the laws of diminishing returns. The fact that increasing returns exist does not mean that diminishing returns do not. Far from it. In his *Harvard Business Review* article, Brian Arthur argues that the two phenomena will always co-exist and are complementary, and that most businesses, especially mature ones, will forever remain in the world of diminishing returns.[94] However, the new thinking about increasing returns helps us understand why high-tech companies, like Intel, Compaq, Microsoft, IBM, Sun Microsystems and Oracle, operate by rules that economists either had long believed impossible or had chosen to ignore.

In his article, Arthur notes that:

In the early days of my work on increasing returns, I was told they were an anomaly. Like some exotic particle in physics, they might exist in theory but would be rare in practice. And if they did exist, they would last for only a few seconds before being arbitraged away. But by the mid-1980s, I realised increasing returns were neither rare nor ephemeral. In fact, a major part of the economy was subject to increasing returns – high technology.[95]

Unsurprisingly then, the concept of increasing returns subliminally hugs the prose of much of Bill Gates's book, *The Road Ahead*, as he expounds his views on the future of high-tech and the computing industry in particular. It finds expression in his references to 'positive feedback'.[96]

Like Bill Gates, Brian Arthur believes increasing returns, or the economic effects of positive feedback, are now permanent features on the economic landscape. This means that those companies who, by dint of competitive shrewdness, outstanding innovation, astute timing or an overwhelmingly marketable product, have stolen a competitive advantage in the marketplace are likely not only to sustain this advantage but to augment it. The chances are that those who are ahead will get further ahead. Positive feedback means that success tends to be automatically reinforced but, contrariwise, loss tends to be accentuated. Arguably, then, increasing returns generate not stability – as, theoretically, does competition in the world of diminishing returns – but instability.

Arthur maintains that this phenomenon, and thus the market instability it causes, will not go away. Increasing returns are not ephemeral. He believes this is so for three reasons summed up in the three phrases: 'up-front costs', 'network effects' and 'customer groove-in'.

One of the distinguishing features of the high-tech industries is their up-front costs – heavy investment in ideas, research and development. Microsoft's Windows NT operating system software is estimated to have cost somewhere in the region of $150 million in R&D costs.[97] However, the cost of reproducing the product, by comparison, is virtually negligible. Indeed, if Microsoft were to change its policy and decide to distribute the software only via the Net, though an unlikely strategy in the short term, this would diminish the cost even further. In the States, where there is no charge for local calls, the cost would be virtually zero. This costing structure contrasts sharply with that of classic economic theory, based as it is on a material world, which assumes that pricing policy is closely correlated to the cost of unit production.

The wealth created by the relatively young company, Netscape, confounds the conventions of both finance and economics. For a company which did not exist in 1993 to achieve a valuation of over $3 billion after its flotation on the stock market is perhaps highly exceptional and impressive. On paper anyway, its owners were millionaires, if not billionaires, almost overnight. This is a far cry from the nineteenth-century stereotype of a millionaire or industrial magnate, like Sir Henry Tate of Tate & Lyle or Sir William Burrell, the ship-owner, who gradually built up their businesses over a lifetime and left legacies in the form of the Tate Gallery and the Burrell Collection.

Fast-forward to the late twentieth century. Netscape's development model confounded conventional thinking on return-on-investment theories and centuries-old models of pricing behaviours and market growth patterns. Installed in an estimated 30 million computers by 1996, a mere two years from inception, Netscape's Navigator Internet browser leapfrogged the reach even of the formerly all-conquering Microsoft. Its ability to do this was determined by strange laws which govern digitisation and software distribution. Netscape transcended the hitherto historical necessity of incurring distribution costs by choosing to distribute its first software product free on the Internet. The only cost – negligible – was the loading of it on to an Internet server. Instantly, this software became available to anybody with Internet access, literally anywhere in the world; all for just the cost of a local phone call, if that, and some patience. There was no manufacturing of computer discs, no millions of printed manuals, no shrink-wrapping, no warehousing, no retail distribution – just the Net. It is surely the first company in history to be worth over $5 billion by giving away its product, metaphorically speaking, on the electronic street corner.

Netscape's ability to pull off this feat did, however, depend on the faith of financiers in its ability to make economic good. The stock market kept faith with Netscape – a necessary prerequisite for its buoyant valuation – and assumed the following: that one day Netscape would introduce a charging policy, which it did; exploit its brand value and corporate goodwill by developing associated products, which it did; and expand its market, which it did. Netscape's wealth creation activities turned conventional economics upside down. For the first time, a company created an almost infinite product inventory without consuming any resources in the form of labour, machinery or transport in the process. And Netscape is not the only company which has defied economic logic, just one of the most spectacular.

In addition to high up-front investment costs and strangely low reproduction costs, Arthur's second idea – 'network externalities' – also holds sway in industries heavy on know-how and light on material resources. In the software industry, for example, this means that the more widely an operating system is used, the higher the probability that it will become an industry standard and, thus, the more people who will want to use it to ensure that their software is compatible with that of other network users. This makes it hard for rivals to compete and shoehorn a competitive toe-hold in the marketplace.

Arthur's third phrase, 'customer groove-in', (or 'customer lock-in') refers to the fact that many high-tech products are highly sophisticated and require customers to commit to a relatively long learning curve in order to maximise their resulting competitive gains. Having invested this learning energy, customers are then loath to switch to a different technology, not least because in a global marketplace driven by adrenaline and adaptability downtime can be costly and major discontinuities crippling.

Arguably then, one can suggest that, taken in concert, the triple effect of 'up-front costs', 'network effects' and 'customer groove-in', lead to unchecked monopolistic tendencies. They may even lead, it seems, to total industry lock-out by the company which has masterminded strategic advantage.

Surely this is not the case? Surely the very nature of competition in knowledge-intensive industries suggests that those who transcend the prevailing paradigm gain competitive advantage? Indeed. Moreover, this is likely to be masterminded by the least expected competitor, that is, by the proverbial upstart, the person labouring all day and all night in their garage or garret, thinking the unthinkable and dreaming the impossible. Is not Netscape the living embodiment of this phenomenon? Well, yes. True, a firm like Microsoft can conquer a market – at least for a time – by exploiting increasing returns, but its ability to abuse its power is limited. Moreover, the advantage of the lock-in effect is tempered by the rapid pace of technological innovation which favours the emergence of new products and thereby opens the door to new entrants. One could argue that lock-in is a strategic disadvantage, a core incompetence even, for as success begets success it increases the temptation to milk it. But often, ironically, strategic advantage will lie in abandoning exactly that success. Difficult to contemplate, far less stomach, but a competitive reality none the less.

In an industry that is 'capital lite' and 'intellect heavy', barriers to entry tend to be determined by access to ideas and knowledge and not to capital in the traditional sense. By definition, this should lower the barriers to entry, enabling anyone with bright ideas to compete. Falling communication costs and the Internet compound this probability. Unlike the aviation, steel or oil industries, knowledge-based industries require little in the way of physical infrastructure. In the past, only large companies could afford the computing infrastructure and the global marketing presence necessary for market advantage, but now small firms can have the same access.

An increasingly light infrastructure reduces the minimum size a firm has to be in order to operate profitably, as overheads are more divisible. Concentration of advantage need not then be harmful in the long run, as long as barriers to entry are low. The mere threat of competition can make a firm behave competitively, as indeed it should. Microsoft, for example, has a near-monopoly in PC software, but it remains innovative because its markets are contestable.

Thus, it would appear that increasing returns do exist as a phenomenon and, as Brian Arthur said, are neither rare nor ephemeral. They are an aspect of the economy that is destined to endure and become more and more pervasive as the information revolution bites. It would appear that increasing returns do not necessarily lead to an inalienable competitive advantage – indeed the very factor that augments returns increases the probability of competition. The logic of increasing returns is not *all* pervasive. Far from it – and the new economic theorists have never wished to deny this; in fact quite the opposite. They acknowledge that the characteristics of diminishing returns, and the dynamic market logic which underpins them, remain highly apposite. However, equally apposite is the law of increasing returns which will increasingly affect and pervade the performance of the knowledge-based industries.

Two Economies: Two Cultures

In his analysis of increasing returns, Brian Arthur goes beyond 'just' a re-assessment of a basic economic principle. He argues that each of those two inter-related worlds – one characterised primarily by diminishing returns and one by increasing returns – exhibits different cultural characteristics, different competitive rhythms, different management techniques and calls for different codes of government regulation. In short, they require a different business mindset.

His view is that industries characterised by diminishing returns inhabit a more ordered world than that of the high-tech industries. The former tend to deal with material production, processing and servicing. Here change is more gradual, the pace less frenetic, production more repetitive, prices more standard, and the parameters less transient. The capital investment in manufacture and distribution is relatively high. These industries are about sustaining high quality and minimising inefficiencies, about constant improvement and constant optimisation.

By contrast the knowledge-based industries are more volatile and advantage is more transient. Here company structure is more dynamic, initiative more likely to delegated, innovation more critical and optimisation a possible disadvantage. In order to promote innovation the company has to operate in small guerrilla-like units linked loosely to the centre. Effectively hierarchy is dissolved. Here repetition is not a means towards optimisation and excellence, but a possible obstacle to innovation.

The consequence, Arthur maintains, of those different characteristics is that the culture and management style which typifies them is radically different. While material industries require a firm and steady hand on the central tiller, lest dissidence upsets a finely-attuned optimising system, virtual industries require a light and distant touch. The latter thrive in an environment that promotes dissidence, autonomy, lateral thinking and challenge to the system.

It would seem, at least to a degree, that Arthur is right. The more a company's competitive position is enhanced by its ability to innovate and to upset the paradigmatic apple-cart, the more its management needs to promote discontinuity and creative energy. Perhaps even materially-based industries now know they will have to re-assess their typically hierarchical 'command and control' type of management. Now communication technology is so pervasive, product life-cycles so reduced, time to market so compressed and the pace of business so generally frenetic, command and control is perhaps too reactive a style. However, these industries cannot afford to be too radical. Strong elements of continuity must undoubtedly remain, not least because of their heavy investment in a physical infrastructure – factories, warehouses, retail outlets. But innovative thinking and fleet-footed operations are also required. Optimisation is no longer necessarily the only way, or indeed a sure way, of keeping ahead of the competition.

Thus material industries, like virtual industries, must work equally hard at eroding complacency. As Michael Grade, chairman of Leisure First and erstwhile CEO of Channel 4, said, when asked about what he perceived to be the greatest enemy of success, 'Complacency, a feeling that we've cracked it, we know that we've got the code now, we know how this works . . . You don't, you absolutely don't.'[98] A similar sentiment was espoused by John Kotter, Konosuke Matsushita Professor of Leadership at the Harvard Business School, when he noted that: 'A majority of employees must believe that considerable change is absolutely necessary.'[99] He urges companies to create a sense of urgency and offers six ways to 'raise the corporate heat'. These are: creating a crisis; eliminating obvious examples of corporate opulence; setting targets so high that they can't be reached by doing business as usual; sharing more information about customer satisfaction and financial performance with employees; insisting that people talk regularly to unsatisfied customers, unhappy suppliers, and disgruntled shareholders; and being more open, direct and honest within the company about the difficulties of the marketplace and the challenges the company faces. As he puts it: 'no more happy talk'.

Amongst other things, this challenges management to be more honest and open about corporate performance and to get out there where the action is and mingle. As Michael Grade puts it: 'You've got to be open, you've got to get out and about, you can't be locked in your office.'[100] For employees and associates, the largest challenge is in rising to meet the new targets and in dealing with the artificially created crisis. Each of those two tactics depends for effect on occasional use. If deployed continuously, their efficacy will rapidly diminish.

So this 'new' economic law of increasing returns, and the concepts of abundance and disequilibrium which underpin it, have noticeable effects on corporate thinking and the corporate mindset. While predictability, sure rhythm, relative stability and optimisation will continue to be observable in material industries, this 'peace' will increasingly be disturbed by the urgency and the unpredictability of the virtual world. This seems inevitable unless consumerism it totally turned on its head: an unlikely event one would think perhaps, indeed, desirable. Globalisation and rapid communication technologies will up the pace and with it, competitive appetites. Consequently, alas, marketing will become more aggressive and customers will be valued more for their anticipated lifelong 'economic value' rather than for their willingness to trade in the here and now. Their perceived future value will matter more than their current being.

A WORLD ON SPEED

We are suffering, not from the rheumatics of old age, but from the growing pains of over-rapid changes, from the painfulness of readjustment between one economic period and another. The increase of technical efficiency has been taking place faster than we can deal with the problem of labour absorption.

A comment on the contemporary scene? No, a quote from John Maynard Keynes in 1930.[101]

If change seemed 'over-rapid' to Keynes in 1930, his ghost should visit the 1990s. Writing back in the 1960s, Alvin Toffler noted that the speed of social, technological and economic change was happening so rapidly that the future would be a constant shock to us all. His message even then was: speed takes its toll.[102]

In 1960 a transatlantic cable could carry 138 conversations simultaneously. In 1996 a fibre-optic cable could carry 1.5 million, and, soon, an optic fibre the diameter of a human hair will be able to transmit across the Atlantic, in less than a second, the content of every issue the *Economist* has ever printed in its 153-year history.[103] Anyone living in the seventeenth century was apparently required to absorb less information in their entire lifetime than we soak up from one issue of a weekday edition of the *New York Times*. And the mushrooming growth in the Internet is another indicator, if we need one, that communications are now happening at lightning speed. Moreover, no communication medium before it has grown so fast.

Meanwhile, the *Guardian* newspaper reported in December 1996 that a $53 million supercomputer, being built out of 7,264 Pentium Pro chips, had broken the computer world speed record by running at 1.06 teraflops, or a trillion floating point operations per second. The previous record, set in September 1996, by a Hitachi supercomputer, was 368 gigaflops, that is 368 billion floating point operations per second. The *Guardian* noted that the world's first teraflops machine was being constructed at Intel's factory in Beaverton, Oregon for America's Sandia National Laboratories in Albuquerque, where it would be used to simulate nuclear explosions.[104]

Driven by Adrenaline

Like the microprocessor industry, the telecommunications industry illustrates in graphic degree the impact of technology and globalisation. Not only can you now call anyone, anywhere in the world, at any time, virtually, but the freefone services which you may dial are, it seems, scattered across the globe irrespective of the caller's location. Globalisation, deregulation, competition, falling telecommunication charges and the application of sophisticated technology mean that firms are siting 'call centres' wherever they choose, outsourcing literally to far flung ends of the Earth, although not outer space – yet. You may be sitting in Toulouse, but your computer technical support person could be sitting in Amsterdam, your 0800 number respondent in Maine, and your Internet service provider helpdesk in Dublin.

Due to the collapsing cost of telecommunications, physical proximity is becoming irrelevant to many activities. Documents, graphics, photographs and videos – all digitised and translated into computer-speak – can travel instantaneously around the world thanks to multimedia communications, sophisticated software and broad bandwidth. Effectively we have created for ourselves a cost effective way to relocate entire chunks of business activity. Digital material can be exported or imported easily. So too, then, can the jobs associated with it. Thus the US insurance company Cigna gets its medical claims processed in Loughrea, Ireland; film production companies in central London receive, edit and re-transit film rushes over digital transatlantic links to and from Hollywood studios; and Bangalore supplies computer programming to Europe and the States via digital networks.

According to the World Bank, the cost of a transatlantic voice call in the year 2000 will be one per cent of what it was in 1987, and by 2010 it will be three cents an hour – next to nothing.[105] Whether this is literally the case or not, the trend is everywhere downwards and will be accelerated as existing protectionist practices are lifted. The implication of this trend is that a sort of global highly competitive tele-economy will be born where the traded product or service is capable of being digitised and thus transmitted electronically. Since all information, news and entertainment forms can be digitised, not only does this trend affect the media and communication industries directly but all business indirectly, for much of business is conducted and transacted through the spoken voice or the written word. The trend is good news for those with the skills to supply the original content or to add value in the transition process, and to hustle for business in this new global arena, but it is not such good news for others. We will not all have the skills, or the disposition, to participate in this competitive rat race.

The combined effect of plunging telecommunication costs and superfast technology is to reduce the cost of transmitting information and speed up the process of communication. The performance of the marketplace therefore approximates more closely to the economic theory of what is termed 'perfect competition', a basic building block of conventional economics. Perfect competition assumes abundant information, zero transaction costs and no barriers to entry. Clearly this is unobtainable in the real world, but as computers and advanced telecommunication technologies converge, we get ever closer to it. Information technology –

and the Internet in particular – makes information on prices, products, goods and services more instantly and easily available. Through digital software agents, it also facilitates the instantaneous comparison of competing prices anywhere on the globe. Better information, low transaction costs and lower barriers to entry all add up to a more efficient and competitive market, and are music to the ears of the perfectionists and the theoreticians. However, for most mortals the difficulty is that such perfection demands a constant peak of efficiency and with it constant change. Rapid and constant oscillations in prices, returns on investment, fees and wages make constant adaptation to the demands of this marketplace a painful experience. This is but one downside to the upside of new technology.

The Downside of the Upside

There are other downsides. In the 1980s an inevitable concomitant of corporate restructuring was corporate fall-out – or so it seemed. By the early 1990s, an apparently invigorating and positive term – re-structuring – had come to signify a rather limited and distinctly dispiriting process: the corporate shedding of labour. Those dispossessed in this way came, understandably, to regard the term with some disdain, if not pronounced distaste.

However, for those who were spared the axe, corporate life, post re-structuring, has hardly been a bed of roses. Far from it. Higher pressures on fewer employees, long hours and high octane activity have undoubtedly taken their toll on our health and well-being. One by-product, or symptom, of this pressurised corporate life is the mountain of paperwork, the multiplicity of meetings, and the excess of communiqués we are expected to deal with, over and above executing the actual tasks for which we were employed. In aspiring to the reality of a paperless environment, we seem to have created a paper-drenched office. We are saturated – satiated – with communiqués of all descriptions. At some point, no doubt, we are going to roll over belly up and declare that enough is enough. It was all a lot simpler when we lived in caves.

The trouble is that, amongst the highly-relevant paperwork, there are cascades of trivia. Like Pugg, the cyber pirate in Stanislaw Lem's science fiction tale, we are engulfed in superfluity: '. . . and it seemed to Pugg that any minute now he would learn of the most fabulous, unheard-of things, things that would open up to him the Ultimate Mystery of Being, so he greedily read everything . . .'[106] Needless to say, Pugg the Pirate never did find the Ultimate Mystery of Being.

When Diane Keaton told her workaholic husband in Woody Allen's film, *Play It Again Sam*, that he should give the office the number of the pay phone they were passing in case they needed him, it was a big joke, but what was farce twenty-five years ago is awesome reality today. The corporate mantra seems to be: have technology, be available. In consequence, if we are not available people think we should be and are frustrated and annoyed if we are not. Ironically, technology applied ostensibly to relieve that frustration, like call forward options and voice messaging, merely serves to escalate the irritation.

An American study of Fortune 1000 companies in 1997, conducted jointly by Gallup, the Institute of the Future and San Jose University, uncovered the degree to which communication mania has taken hold.[107] The study revealed that an average middle-management executive sends or receives 178 messages or documents a day, including 56 phone calls, 23 e-mail messages, 21 voice-mail messages, 15 faxes, 14 Post-it note messages, 13 phone message slips and 11 inter-office/internal mail. Many of those have absolutely no relevance whatsoever to the executive concerned. Although the study looked at 1,000 of the largest international companies, it warned that the problems would soon pervade companies of all sizes. It noted that a gridlock is emerging which makes it even harder to get the attention of the recipient. As employees become frustrated at not being able to get through, they send the same message several times by different channels, thus creating even more traffic. The same kind of ironic sentiments and behaviour patterns exist in the UK as well.

And so we come to a rather peculiar impasse. With the growth of communications, it seems, people expect others to be more available for them, but at the same time they are desperate to be less available themselves. A type of corporate snobbery has taken hold. Symptomatic of such misplaced disdain is the situation where the caller assumes that if you can spend three minutes on the phone without interruption from another call then you must be a 'sad' case of a side-stepped executive in want of a life. Being constantly engaged and effectively unobtainable signifies status and position.

We all know how frustrating it is always to get a voice message, and how nightmarish it is to meet a succession of automated voice messages forcing you to listen to a series of mostly irrelevant options. So, ironically, we find ourselves in a rather Kafkaesque situation. We have more and more devices for contacting people than ever before, but seem to spend our time trying, and failing, to connect. Perhaps, like motorways and the Internet, the secret is to look for ways of purposely reducing the traffic carried rather than increasing it. Perhaps solitude rather than connectivity will be the balm for our soul in the twenty-first century. Swimming against the tide, and in search of such solitude, some individuals are taking direct and individual action. They are literally unhooking themselves from technology. One of them is Peter Suedfeld, Professor of Psychology at the University of British Columbia who specialises in 'solitude' and believes in saying no. His answer phone says cordially, 'I am away, don't leave a message. Search for moments of wonder in your day.'[108]

Perhaps we need the sanctity of solitude more than we realise. In his book *The Third Wave*, Alvin Toffler describes this techno-logical wave (succeeding the agricultural and industrial waves) as a 'powerful tide surging across the world', bewildering business executives as they swim against highly erratic technological and economic currents.

> Old ways of thinking, old formulas, dogmas and ideologies, no matter how cherished or how useful in the past, no longer fit the facts. The world that is fast emerging from the clash of new values and technologies, new geopolitical relationships, new lifestyles and modes of communications, demands wholly new ideas and analogues, classifications and concepts. We cannot cram the embryonic world of tomorrow into yesterday's conventional cubbyholes.[109]

In a similar vein, Don Tapscott, author of *The Digital Enterprise*, sub-titled *Promise and Peril in the Age of Networked Intelligence*, observes that: 'We are at the dawn of the age of networked intelligence – an age that is giving birth to a new economy, a new politics, and a new society. Businesses will be transformed, governments will be renewed and individuals will be able to reinvent themselves.' Equally, he is aware of the perils of such a networked economy maintaining that: 'A looming dark side holds the potential of severe social stratification, unprecedented invasion of privacy and other rights, structural unemployment and massive social dislocation and conflict.'[110]

Professor Ian Angell of the London School of Economics foresees 'an age of rage'.[111] Many, he predicts, especially those not in the 'new elite', will face discontinuity, uncertainty and dislocation. The elite he sees as forming perhaps 10 per cent of society. They will be the skilled knowledge workers, mercenary in their choice of places to live, connected via a network and with the full panoply of teleworking technology at their command. As markets become totally global, traditional jobs will be lost on an unprecedented scale. In this scenario, the ghost of mass unemployment will haunt the unskilled. In contrast, the ultra-mobile elite will be welcome anywhere in the world.

Professor Angell believes technological development will destroy the traditional nation state and the conventional company. Corporations will be 'virtualised' or 'vapourised', consisting largely of loosely-knit alliances bound together by cyber-connectivity. Private Internet currencies, perhaps stored electronically on satellites, will curtail the tax-raising capacity of national governments. In Europe in particular, in stark contrast to Asia and South America where the population profile is emphatically young, this problem will be compounded by an ageing population presenting governments with a fiscal nightmare. This, it is feared, will lead to an unprecedented fragmentation of the international structure of countries and nation-states as we know them today. Insofar as companies use the Internet to disappear into cyberspace – a new 'off-shore' tax haven – it will be impossible to derive revenue from them. In these circumstances, the whole economic infrastructure upon which national governments depend for their viability and *raison d'être* will be eroded.

Thus it is predicted that in the twenty-first century economic identity will no longer reside in the geographical architecture of the nation-state, but will mutate and migrate to regional zones of high connectivity and to 'smart' cities. Richer areas will neglect poorer ones, and knowledge workers will move to economically-viable hot spots similar to Hong Kong, Palo Alto, Singapore or the Malaysian Super Corridor. Angell sees the medieval city-state structure as the precedent for such smart zones, which will be served not by the trade routes of old – like for example the old Silk Road which passed from China through Central Asia, India, Persia and the Arab dynasties and then on to Europe – but by hubs of electronic commerce. Instead of the Chinese explorer Zhang Qian, who used silk to open up communications between East and West, we have the Malaysians, Dr Mahathir bin Mohamad and Azznam Shariffadeen, who are using digital technology to open up new cyber-routes between Asia, Europe and the Americas.

The possible bifurcation of rich and poor offers a dismal prognosis. While it offers lucrative rewards for a small minority, it appears to offer the large majority a future of uncertainty, dysfunctionality, turmoil and angst – hardly a basis for social cohesion and communal harmony. However, other social commentators, like Toffler, offer hope for a brighter future beyond our present period of transition, providing of course that we embrace the 'crashing waves of technical change'. Meanwhile, Charles Leadbeater in his paper, *Britain: the California of Europe*, believes we can embrace the upside of this technological change. He cites California as a model of a knowledge-intensive, networked economy that the UK might choose to emulate. He argues for a silicon transplant to turn Britain into the California of Europe, successfully diversified from declining 'smokestack' industries into a hive of information technology companies.[112]

In 1996, California was home to approximately 22 per cent of all US high-tech jobs, in about 6,000 high-tech companies, all concentrated in Silicon Valley, the narrow strip of land wedged between Palo Alto in the west and San Jose in the south. In 1996, venture capitalists invested more than $2 billion dollars in small companies in Silicon Valley which has its own GDP of about $65 billion, about the same as Chile's 15 million inhabitants, according to CCSCE.[113] Leadbeater points out that California, similar in size to the UK, has been more successful than any other Western economy in restructuring away from the old, declining industries and into computers, the Internet, biotechnology, tourism, multimedia entertainment and design. He notes that information technology is at the forefront of California's new economy in which 'soft' intellectual assets such as creativity, knowledge, ideas and branding will play a far more important role in generating growth than the 'hard' physical assets of land, manual labour and machinery. Although the UK lacks the advantages of a vista on to the Pacific and extra-strong trading relationships with Asian

Pacific Rim economies, it has a sterling history and a compelling presence in the worlds of design, fashion, music, broadcasting, film production, publishing and tourism. Nurturing these soft assets as it does, arguably the UK offers fertile ground for growth well into the next century.

However, like the Californian economy, if not indeed the whole world economy, the UK faces a key social and economic challenge. Assuming the labour force will be displaced to the extent envisaged, how will we engage the economically disenfranchised? Despite California's digital prosperity, it continues to suffer from wide social and economic inequalities expressed in poverty, racism, violence, intolerance and crime. It raises the spectre of a frighteningly disaffected underbelly. Science fiction writers like William Gibson have explored this dichotomous future and expose their own personal ambivalence in the process. Gibson in fact has been quoted as saying that nanotechnology gives him 'the creeps'.

Many of us are worried, for few really positive futures have been painted for those of us – and there are lots of us – on the fringes of this high-tech loop. Jeremy Rifkin, in his book bleakly entitled *The End of Work*, offers a version of state-run charitable work as a bulwark against quasi-Gibsonian nightmares in which the erstwhile middle class has vanished and the minute techno-elite is supported by an obsolete underclass.[114] These are fearful, and ultimately negative, visions. In the interests of social justice, human dignity and indeed international stability, we need to search far more urgently for positive options. We need to find hope and ignite ambition. If our digital future is to yield prosperity and ooze contentment, we need to place economic viability and social capability in the hands of the overwhelming majority, not just in the palm of a privileged elite.

REGIONAL HOT SPOTS

Perhaps as well as looking west and to California for inspiration, the UK needs to look east, for one of the brightest lights in the infotech firmament is Asia. Silicon Valley may well be the high-tech fashion centre, but it's not the only market, nor the most dynamic. While Europe remains a centre of considerable innovation and a key international market, Asia boasts eight out of the world's ten fastest growing econimies – plus the still largely untapped markets of China and India[115] – and Japan and Korea bring internationally established and shrewd business expertise. More than half of the world's population of 2.5 billion who are under the age of 20 reside in Asia. This fact alone points strongly to Asia's economic potential in the twenty-first century. Coupled with its economic dynamism, as demonstrated by Japan and Korea, this means the region and its entrepreneurs may one day play the leading role in creating and driving the technological innovation which is at the heart of the information revolution. Thus what Britain was to the Industrial Revolution, Asia may very well be to the Digital Revolution.

Seeing this potential, politicians and entrepreneurs in select parts of Asia have invested heavily in the infrastructure which will pave the way for electronic commerce and a digitally-based economy. Since 1991, Singapore officials have invested over $2 billion in a state-of-the-art technology infrastructure to build one of the world's first 'intelligent islands'. Combined with a highly-rated telecommunications system, this is clearly attracting international companies – among them Citibank, Hewlett Packard and Reuters – to use the Singaporian infrastructure as their regional data hub and thus to be ushered into Singapore's digital fold.

However, perhaps the government which has been the boldest in creating silicon age opportunities for its citizens is that of Malaysia. It aims to leapfrog the industrial age and move straight into the information age, with the creation of Cyberjaya, the 'virtual city'. Though virtually connected, Cyberjaya will be very real. It will be part of an area south of Kuala Lumpur, designated the Multimedia Super Corridor or MSC, and stretching from the Twin Towers at the centre of Kuala Lumpur in the north to the new international airport at Sepang in the south. Cyberjaya will be the MSC city for industry, research institutes, the Multimedia University and international corporations. A second city, Putrajaya (the 'intelligent' capital), yet to be built, will be the new administrative capital for Malaysia. Due to open in 1998, the Super Corridor is 15km by 50km: an area larger than Singapore.

While the Malaysian government can provide the physical infrastructure, it realises that if it is to effect the transition from an almost pre-industrial economy to a post-industrial economy, it needs to commandeer talent beyond its own national boundaries. Like the science parks and tax-free enterprise zones of the West, designed to stimulate innovation and enterprise, MSC will lift visa restrictions for skilled multimedia operators and encourage the inflow of fresh, internationally skilled talent. Every home in the residential areas, termed 'cybervillages' and yet to be built, will be connected via a 2.5 to 10 GB (gigabyte) optic fibre network. This will link the corridor directly with other ASEAN countries, Japan, Europe and the USA. Arif Nun, the project's chief operating officer, dreams of a new global community living in the corridor, flying in and out of Sepang airport, and criss-crossing the globe.

In order to develop the idea of the super corridor a lot of criss-crossing has already occurred. Malaysia knows it lacks the capacity to realise the corridor on its own. This is part of the reason that it has scoured the world for the necessary technological know-how and the corporate connections. The American firm, McKinsey, is acting as consultant and has seconded advisers from the USA, Germany, India, China and Hong Kong to work in Kuala Lumpur. The international advisory panel is informed by the same spirit. Its twenty-nine members represent a *Who's Who* of Silicon Valley and include Louis Gerstner from IBM, James Clark from Netscape, Bill Gates from Microsoft, Noboru Miyawaki from Nippon Telegraph and Telephone (NTT), Kenichi Ohmae from the University of California at Los Angeles (UCLA) and Toyko, and Eckhard Pfeiffer from Compaq.

What sets Malaysia's multimedia corridor apart from the business park developments of the West is its scale and the breadth of the vision behind it. The boldness is breathtaking. Asian 'tigers' have faced obstacles in trying to close the gap on the West, but one of their advantages is that with no industrial legacy they can at least start afresh with state-of-the-art technology. By 2000, Malaysia plans to have the world's first national multi-purpose smart card containing each citizen's identity card information and electronic signature, enabling direct access to government, banking, credit, telephone, transport and club services. Several new cyberlaws have already been adopted, including ones relating to digital signatures, digital contracts and the protection of digital intellectual assets. 'Smart schools' are planned where teachers will concentrate on developing the potential of the right-hand side of the brain, the creative side. As the Malaysian leaders say, educating the left-hand side of the brain can be automated. They also plan to incorporate telemedicine as a way of transforming the standards of healthcare and combining the best of Chinese Ayuredic medicine with the best of Western medical knowledge. This is the bold vision of Azznam Shariffadeen whose thinking inspired the Super Corridor. No wonder enthusiasts refer to all this as 'an outrageous opportunity'.

It's outrageous, too, because of the 'reckless' speed of its implementation – or at least so it appears to Western eyes. The organising and initiating body, the National Information Technology Council, was established in 1994 and by August 1995 the proposal had received the blessing of Prime Minister Dr Mahathir bin Mohamad who launched it, fittingly, in a ceremony held in the middle of the jungle. There was something bizarre about this. It seems odd that a country emerging from an agrarian economy with almost undignified haste should have concertinaed its industrialisation phase into a mere twenty years. Europe 'spun it out' over one hundred and fifty. In the 1960s, the Malaysian economy was still highly dependent on palm oil, rubber and tin. In the 1970s and 1980s, the country launched itself on the road to industrialisation at breakneck speed. Realising though that the goalposts had moved, Malaysia has sought to make a virtue out of its lack of an industrial infrastructure, and catapult itself into the digital future. While all great transitions are not without turmoil and elements of failure and disaffection, the impact of Malaysia's visionary gamble with modernity should not be underestimated. This bold blueprint will affect us all.

IMPLANTING CAPACITY

Evidently Malaysia has set its sights on the future and a rise to economic prominence in the twenty-first century, but equally, the West is not without its silicon age aspirations. It is intent on sustaining its competitive edge, and nowhere is this more apparent than in the nature and extent of its digital R&D investments. The research agendas of the world's top-ranking computer science labs – Carnegie, Mellon, Stanford, MIT and Edinburgh, to name but a few – and their interwoven links with industry, point to a strategic intention to remain at the sharpest edge of the cutting edge. Peering behind the lab doors, we can begin to get a feel for the future, for in fifteen, or perhaps twenty years' time, the research projects of today will be the innovative applications of tomorrow and will have permeated the mainstream of our economy.

How can we be so sure that today's research focus will be tomorrow's industrial application? There are two reasons. First the magnitude of the momentum and the energy behind the various research programmes makes its unlikely that they will be stopped in their tracks. Indeed, the process of dissemination out of the research lab and into the marketplace is already in train. The stable doors have already opened. Second, the fact that the seeds of research are spread so widely across so many labs makes innovation virtually inevitable.

The movement towards miniaturisation and faster speeds shows no signs of abating either in industry or in the research lab. Indeed, it may even be accelerating. Microchip manufacturers ship about 3.5 billion 'embedded' or 'invisible' real-time microprocessors every year: that is, microchips dedicated to a specific task or group of tasks, and embedded in devices and applications other than computers.[116] That amounts to fifty times as many as are hard-wired into computers. Already microchips permeate our lives, perhaps more than we realise. They are in the microwave, the VCR, and the car's anti-locking brakes system for example.

Most digital pioneers agree that this trend towards miniaturisation and pervasiveness will, in the near future, be accelerated to the point where computing power becomes ubiquitous and complex technology is even more deftly disguised in simple operations. David St Charles, president and CEO of Integrated Systems Inc. (ISI), the $100 million market leader among embedded systems developers, describes his business as one centred on 'invisibility'. It's what he does for a living, he claims: making technology 'disappear'. ISI technology is deeply embedded in many industrial products, for instance, in Kodak and Xerox printers and photocopiers, Motorola communication satellites, Hewlett Packard interactive TV set-top boxes and Boeing planes.

While the research agendas in the computer labs are both wide-ranging and multi-dimensional, there seems to be a common thrust to all the R&D programmes: electronic engineers, scientists and software developers are all looking for ways to make computing more intuitive and modelled more on organic processes. Amongst some scientists, a whole new metaphor for computing is taking shape, patterned on the natural resilience and elegance of biological organisms. Researchers at the University of California in San Diego, for example, are investigating the possibility of using a green fluorescent protein, the one which controls a jellyfish's glow, as the replacement material for the microprocessor's silicon base. They foresee the possibility that computer memory systems could, in future, store data in genetically engineered 'fluorescent' protein molecules.[117]

Researchers observe the astonishing ease with which living systems process staggering volumes of sensory data. If such an ability can be fabricated and embedded in microchips, they conjecture, then the machines of the future may 'learn' to diagnose, repair and even replicate themselves. One of the most cutting edge technologies on show at the fourth European Conference on Artificial Life in 1997 was 'evolvable hardware'. This, as the term suggests, incorporates computer chips that borrow lessons from biology to 'evolve', apparently, without human intervention. Almost one hundred and eighty years since Mary Shelley wrote *Frankenstein*, the European Conference underlined how far this burgeoning area of research had developed beyond the imagination of science fiction writers. One exhibit was a purple spider-like machine 'with a mind of its own' that liked to go walkabout.[118] We must hope and trust its tag, 'Frankenstein's successor', will turn out to be wholly inappropriate.

The Media Lab at the Massachusetts Institute of Technology (MIT) has been closely associated both with the inspiration of its Director, Nicholas Negroponte, and with its artificial intelligence research programme. Negroponte believes that escaping from present cultures, expectations and prejudices is what keeps the Media Lab alive, as does a healthy does of 'craziness'. This 'craziness' is best epitomised by the 'MIT Things that Think' research programme which is investigating future interfaces for computing. Researchers, amazingly, see prodigious potential in surfaces and textures which most of us regard as quintessentially mundane: for instance, the lining of our jackets, our shoulder pads or the heels of our shoes – 'the most underexploited part of everyday clothing' according to Negroponte.

Central to this 'crazy' vision is the use of the human body as the network that links the computers of tomorrow together. What MIT refers to as 'body area networks', IBM calls 'personal area networks' (PANs), and has demonstrated the potential of two business executives exchanging a business card's worth of personal information simply by shaking hands. Both must carry card-size transmitters and receivers. Their handshake then completes an electric circuit, and each person's data is transferred to the other's laptop computer. While such a small gesture is unspectacular, it does demonstrate the potential of the technology and the future of our very own, and highly personal, 'area networks'.

If this still seems a bit futuristic, consider Peter Cochrane's observation, that as surgeons have performed thousands of cochlear implants on patients with hearing loss, these people are already walking around with 'chips' in their heads. As Head of Research at British Telecom (BT), he is close to the leading edge of new technology. Meanwhile researchers at BT predict that future generations of portable phones could be installed right in your ear. While talking, the user could also glimpse images or data that are pulled invisibly off the Internet and projected on to a magnifying mirror positioned beside one eye.[119] Our high-tech future, it seems, is all about miniaturisation, mathematics and silicon expertise. The combination of speed, power and minuscularity will usher in a more pervasive and invisible micro presence in our homes and offices such that by 2020 it will be hard to find any object that is not wired.

One of the technologies driving this trend is nanotechnology which deals with machines built of molecules rather than metal parts and with dimensions of a billionth of a metre. Many research teams are exploring the potential of this shrunken-down world. One such is in the department of electrical and electronic engineering at the University of Leeds, under the direction of Professor Snowden who foresees that the next wave of supercomputing may be based on gallium arsenide, not on silicon as is the current microprocessor. The Leeds team has been working with combinations of indium gallium arsenide and a new material called indium phosphide which permit smaller machines and higher frequencies. Today's Pentium processors, for example, work at up to 200MHz. With nanotechnology such as that being explored at Leeds we are talking about 10,000 or 100,000 times higher than that.

As an indication of this minuscule world, scientists at Cornell University in America have unveiled the world's smallest 'guitar' – twenty times thinner than a human hair and just ten micrometres long, one micrometre being one-millionth of a metre. Using nanotechnology, it was carved out of crystal silicon and is no longer than a blood cell while each of its strings is 100 atoms across, or 4,000 times thinner than a human hair. The six-string instrument can be played by using the tip of an atomic force microscope, but any noise, alas, cannot be heard by the human ear. The potential of this area of technological development for industrial application was illustrated by the report, *Making It In Miniature*, which estimated that by the year 2000, nanotechnology could represent an £80 billion worldwide market.[120] Smallness, it seems, will be everything and will be a highly fertile area of R&D. In fact it will pervade our industrial fabric in the next ten to twenty years just as raw energy does today. For the diffusion of computer expertise will speed the quest for new metaphors in computing. So will fast communications and the freewheeling scientific anarchy of the Web. Driven by adrenaline and fuelled by intellect this development, and its business ramifications, will undoubtedly be one of the key factors in economic growth over the next twenty-five years.

THE ENTERPRISE CHALLENGE

An indicator of the extent to which business has invested in digital technology is the energy with which it now seeks to safeguard its digital assets. The risks of hacking, fraud, computer failure and legal action in cyberspace are now regarded as sufficiently threatening to make virtual insurance essential. Insurance companies, like bankers and venture capitalists, have always been familiarly comfortable with the world of atoms. Now that the world of 'bits' is upon us, insurance companies are taking pains to understand digital technology, and computer companies are turning their attention to the issues which exercise insurance firms.

Both parties understand that the *status quo* was designed for yesterday and yesterday's loss prevention approaches and insurance responses simply no longer fit. A major rethink of the way insurance companies assess risk is required. For their part, companies operating in cyberspace need to be aware that any online business is automatically exposed to the threats of software infiltration, contamination and adulteration. Therefore, security has to be a major focus of collaboration. Insurance can protect businesses from financial loss, but real protection can only be achieved with increased awareness of net security exposures and concrete loss-control methods to contain them.

However, virtual insurance is just one of the issues which digital companies of today have to grapple with. Take, for instance, company structure: there is a whole list of 'how' issues: how hierarchical or how horizontal; how compact or how dispersed; how spaced-in and how spaced-out; how outsourced and how insourced; how disconnected or how connected; and how virtual and how real? A related issue is centred on synthesising the company's real value chain with its virtual value chain in such a way that added-value is maximised. And what about attracting talent? Issues here include which incentive and reward structure should be adopted with what degree of permanence or temporality; how can the right balance be struck between continuity and intermittency; and, what degree of association should be pursued with employees, partners, contractors and associates?

Then again, how should a company value and safeguard its assets, and indeed, how should it determine which assets are proprietary to its core and which are to be shared with employees, associates, customers, partners and suppliers? Finally, there is the issue of how to promote customer relations. This encompasses two sub-issues: first, how to present and sustain a clear identity and a single point of accountability to the customer – that is, how to avoid the dissipation of responsibility and the dilution of brand essence through partnerships, sub-contracting relationships, franchises and alliances – and second, how to promote the company product or service vigorously whilst respecting and upholding the customer's privacy.

These are just a few of the many issues which are exercising our business leaders. On a more individual level they, and we, must develop a means to sustain a sense of perspective, for the future will be bumpy and lumpy. We must therefore value the art of reflection. Further, we must value the balm of tranquillity, the richness of diversity, the vitality of fun and the sanity of balance – in short, we must have a life – for only then can we ride ambiguity with exhilaration, be open to the lateral view and develop vision with clarity. Moreover, we must seek out ways to deal with overload lest we, like Pugg, the afore-mentioned 'cyberpirate', are engulfed by noise and minutiae. In information terms, we must seek to live a minimalist life adopting the habit of the ultra selective and the super discriminatory. Slivers and *only* slivers of information are what we need and what we must demand – constantly.

On another level, if business is to flourish and the economy create wealth, then it is essential that social entrepreneurship is promoted and sound stability sustained. One of the characteristics which makes the UK so attractive as a location for inward investment is its economic and social stability. A democratic framework and a tradition of social tolerance are essential ingredients in the creation of a milieu which is attractive to entrepreneurs and to artists, artisans, the independently-minded, the progressive and the avant-garde. If we wish to attract the wealth creators of tomorrow, then we must provide a milieu which is convivial to the virtual artisans of today – but this must also provide a socially and economically viable niche for the majority who are, by definition, the 'non-elite'. For without societal stability, the prospects for enduring enterprise and creativity are inevitably limited.

If new technology demands continual change and discontinuity, where do we find sanctuary and peace – a place devoid of the harassments of modern life? In a poignant article entitled 'Pulling up home roots' and catching the *gestalt* of the moment, writer Larry Elliott refers to the twin forces of a globalised market and new technology, and how they have put paid to the idea of a job for life. He notes how comparatively little research there has been about 'how the modern economy runs counter to the need to be rooted, to have a centrality of existence, to have a sense of place . . . [Who] really wants to be part of the new globalised economy if it means living in a state of constant existential fear?'[121] Who indeed?

As justice demands eternal vigilance, so technology requires a constant counterpoise. Just as we must always be alert lest rights be eroded, justice be diminished or responsibility be compromised, we must always temper technology. Otherwise it may deprive us, inadvertently, of the very qualities which make life worth living. Technology is neutral. It is we who decide how to deploy it. The future of our businesses, of our economy and of the fabric of society lies in our hands and in our hands alone. The future is not a destination, it is a process, and it is we – business executives, politicians, planners and citizens – who direct that process. We decide not only what wealth we shall create, but what values we shall live by. Thus, it is we who are responsible for the digital future of tomorrow. This is both a privilege and a challenge.

References

1. 'The triumph of the new economy', *Business Week*, 30 December 1996.
2. Tran, M. and Phillips, T., 'The geek shall inherit the Earth', *The Guardian*, Online section, 20 March 1997.
3. As quoted in *Ibid*.
4. 'Computers and Chips', High Technology, 1997 Industry Outlook, *Business Week*, 13 January 1997.
5. 'The Best Performers', The Business Week Fifty, *Business Week*, 24 March 1997.
6. Schofield, J., 'The invisible billionaire', *The Guardian*, Online section, 13 February 1997.
7. As quoted in 'The Best Performers', The Business Week Fifty, *Business Week*, 24 March 1997.
8. Schlender, B., 'Software hardball. Here's $2 billion. Now go invent', *Fortune*, 30 September 1996.
9. Tran, M. and Phillips, T., 'The geek shall inherit the Earth', *The Guardian*, Online section, 20 March 1997.
10. Kavanagh, J., 'The future is contracted, at £1,000 a week', *The Times*, Interface section, 28 May 1997.
11. Schlender, B., 'Software is everywhere', *Fortune*, 10 June 1996.
12. Port, O., with Reinhardt, A., McWilliams, G., and Brull, S., 'The Silicon Age? It's just dawning', *Business Week*, 9 December 1996.
13. Port, O., 'Gordon Moore's crystal ball', Into the Wild Frontier, Information Technology Annual Report, *Business Week*, 23 June 1997.
14. Schlender, B., 'Software is everywhere', *Fortune*, 10 June 1996.
15. Sillitoe, A., *Saturday Night and Sunday Morning*, W.H. Allen, London, 1958.
16. Lodge, D., *Nice Work*, Secker & Warburg, London, 1988.
17. Schofield, J., 'A tiny sliver not to be sneezed at', *The Guardian*, Online section, 31 October 1996.
18. Internet Communities, Special Report, *Business Week*, 5 May 1996.
19. Tabizel, D., and Rosen, N., *The Internet in 1996: An Investment Perspective*, Durlacher Multimedia, London, 1996.

191

20. Pearce, F., *The Provision of Consumer Online and Internet Services Across Europe*, Datamonitor, London, 1996.
21. As quoted at *The Red Herring* Web site at http://www.herring.com, January 1997.
22. Newbold, L., *Consumer Online Shopping, a European Report*, Datamonitor, London, 1997.
23. *Retail On-line Advances*, Money & Technology Report, Forrester Research, USA, 1996.
24. 'US Web ad market revs up', *New Media Age*, 26 June 1997, with reference to a report by the Internet Advertising Bureau.
25. As quoted in 'US Internet economy to explode by 2000', *Multimedia Business Analyst*, a *Financial Times* Telecoms & Media Publishing newsletter (now *Digital Media Investor*), 11 December 1996.
26. As quoted in 'Now the Net will fit into your pocket', *Sunday Times*, Innovation section, 1 September 1996.
27. Upton, D., and McAfee, A., 'The Real Virtual Factory', *Harvard Business Review*, July–August 1996.
28. 1997 Industry Outlook, Software, Prognosis 1997, *Business Week*, 13 January 1997.
29. *Ibid.*
30. Ohmae, K., *The End of the Nation State: The Rise of Regional Economies*, HarperCollins Publishers, London, 1995.
31. Groves, A., *Only the Paranoid Survive: How to exploit the crisis points that challenge every company and career*, HarperCollins Publishers, London, 1997.
32. Hammond, R., *Digital Business: Surviving and thriving in an on-line world*, Hodder & Stoughton, London, 1996.
33. Partridge, C., 'Another brick in the techno-wall', *The Times*, Interface section, 9 July 1997.
34. 'An acknowledged trend', The World Economy Survey, *Economist*, 28 September 1996.
35. *Ibid.*
36. *The Knowledge-Based Economy*, OECD Conference papers, Copenhagen, 1994, HMSO, 1996.
37. Stewart, T.A., 'Brain Power: Who owns it . . . how they profit from it', *Fortune*, 17 March 1997.
38. As quoted in *Ibid.*
39. Hamel, G., 'Strategy as Revolution', *Harvard Business Review*, July–August 1996.
40. Peppers, D., and Rogers, M., 'Back to the 1:1 future', *New Media Age*, 21 November 1996, and in *The One to One Future: Building relationships one customer at a time*, Doubleday, 1994.
41. Thomas, D., 'Television by numbers', *Financial Times*, 2 December 1996.
42. *Ibid.*
43. As quoted in 'Fly me to the moon', *Creation*, March 1997.
44. Gens, F., 'Predictions 97', *New Media Age*, 9 January 1997.
45. Taylor, P., 'Whirlwind of change in the digital era', Information Technology Review, *Financial Times*, 5 March 1997.

46. As quoted in *Ibid*.

47. Quoted from an interview by Henning, K., with Stewart, F., in October 1996.

48. 'Webcasters aim for recognition as new body holds first meeting', *New Media Age*, 5 June 1997.

49. Shepard, A.C., 'Webward Ho!', *American Journalism Review*, March 1997.

50. Henning, K., 'The sharp end of the cutting edge', *Broadcast*, 19 May 1995.

51. Wyver, J., 'TV21: the survivor's guide', *The Television Book*, Delegates Handbook, Edinburgh International Television Festival, 1994.

52. *Ibid*.

53. Kavanagh, J., 'Banking on the online future', *The Times*, Interface section, 2 July 1997.

54. *Retail Internet Banking: A Survey of Current and Future Development*, Booz.Allen and Hamilton, London, 1996.

55. *Distribution in Retail Banking – A change in style*, KPMG, London, 1997.

56. As quoted in Ryle, S., 'Royal Bank hopes to pick up big profit at Tesco', *Guardian*, 8 May 1997.

57. Treanor, J., 'How virtual banks are close to becoming reality', *Independent*, 21 February 1997.

58. *The Information Superhighway and Retail Banking*, Volume 1, US Bank Administration Institute and the Boston Consulting Group, USA, 1996.

59. *Retail Internet Banking: A Survey of Current and Future Development*, Booz.Allen and Hamilton, London, 1996.

60. As quoted in Utley, T., 'Microsoft's Bill Gates sees his shares double', *Daily Telegraph*, 15 February 1997.

61. Kehoe, L., 'Determined to Dominate', Technology in the Office section, Information Technology supplement, *Financial Times*, 6 November 1996.

62. As quoted in Alexander, G., 'Netscape losing browser battle', *Sunday Times*, Business section, 13 October 1996.

63. *The Internet and Intranet Report*, Zona Research, USA, 1995.

64. Wheelwright, G., and Kehoe, L., 'Gates casts his lines for a Net profit', *Financial Times*, 21 October 1996.

65. Thomson, R., 'Baron Bill casts his media Net', *Sunday Express*, 5 January 1997.

66. As quoted in Snoddy, R., 'Poised to encircle the globe', *Financial Times*, 24 December 1996.

67. Harris, C., 'BT still hanging on the line over MCI', *Financial Times*, 23 July 1997.

68. Hall, A., 'BT soaks up the sun', *Sunday Telegraph*, 20 April 1997.

69. Stoll, C., *Silicon Snake Oil: Second Thoughts on the Information Highway*, Doubleday, USA, 1995.

70. As quoted in Taylor, P., 'Whirlwind of change in the digital era', Information Technology Review, *Financial Times*, 5 March 1997.

71. Barnatt, C., *Cyberbusiness: Mindsets for a Wired Age*, John Wiley & Sons Ltd, 1995.

72. Chesbrough, H.W. & Teece, D.J., 'When is Virtual Virtuous? Organising for Innovation', *Harvard Business Review*, January – February 1996.

73. Elliott, L., 'Pulling up home roots', *Guardian*, 7 July 1997.
74. Riewoldt, O., 'Dream Works', *Independent*, Magazine section, 31 May 1997.
75. Taylor, P., 'The momentum is building rapidly', Information Technology supplement, *Financial Times*, 7 May 1997.
76. As quoted in *Ibid*.
77. Knipe, M., 'This is Sandy Gall, reporting from the desert', Global Communications Focus, *The Times*, 26 March 1997.
78. 'Unlink down under', Global Communications Focus, *The Times*, 26 March 1997.
79. 'Browser war is over as Netscape reinvents itself', *Daily Telegraph*, 22 October 1996.
80. 'Multi-Function Smart Cards', *The Times*, Interface section, 23 October 1996.
81. 'Hardware to wear', *The Times*, Interface section, 30 October 1996.
82. 'Wristwatch telephone', *Sunday Times*, Innovation section, 25 August 1996.
83. Hadland, G., 'Feat of clay starts a new China syndrome', and 'Designer ware on sale to a digital high street', *The Times*, Interface section, 23 April 1997.
84. Partridge, C., 'All aboard for a trip on tomorrow's train', *The Times*, Interface section, 2 July 1997.
85. Morgan, I., 'The new car's great in theory, but will the factory be able to build it?', *The Times*, Car 97 supplement, 26 April 1997.
86. 'Bugs Bunny moves to cyberspace', *Sunday Times*, Innovation section, 16 March 1997.
87. Kleiser, J., As quoted from his presentation, *Daily Telegraph*, Internet '97 conference, 24 June 1997.
88. Taylor, P., 'Fuelling the electronic commerce revolution', Information Technology supplement, *Financial Times*, 7 May 1997.
89. *Intranet Report 1997*, Durlacher, London, 1997: executive summary on Web at http://www.durlacher.com, autumn 1997.
90. *EMC Technology Forecasts: 1998*, Price Waterhouse Entertainment, Media and Communications Group, client publication, 1997: summary on Web at http://www.pricewaterhouse.com. autumn 1997.
91. Nairn, G., 'Fresh opportunities emerge on the Web', Virtual Reality section, Information Technology supplement, *Financial Times*, 7 May 1997.
92. Gilder, G., *Microcosm: The Quantum Revolution in Economics and Technology*, Touchstone Books, USA, 1990.
93. Aley, J., 'The theory that made Microsoft', *Fortune*, 29 April 1996.
94. Arthur, W.B., 'Increasing returns and the new world of business', *Harvard Business Review*, July–August 1996.
95. *Ibid*.
96. Gates, W.H., with Myhrvold, N. and Rinearson, P., *The Road Ahead*, Penguin Books, 1996
97. 'The economics of ideas', *Wired*, August 1996.
98. As quoted in 'How I Made the Grade', *Guardian*, 26 May 1997 (an

edited extract from Lewis, M., *Reflections on Success*, Lennard Publishing, June 1997).

99. Kotter, J.P., 'Killing Complacency', *Fortune*, 5 August 1996.

100. 'How I Made the Grade', *Guardian*, 26 May 1997 (an edited extract from Lewis, M., *Reflections on Success*, Lennard Publishing, June 1997).

101. 'Stop the world, I want to get off', A Survey of the World Economy, *Economist*, 28 September 1996.

102. Alvin Toffler, A., *Future Shock*, Bantam Books, New York, 1970.

103. Woodall, P., 'The Hitchhiker's guide to Cybernomics, A Survey of the World Economy', *Economist*, 28 September 1996.

104. Schofield, J., 'Netwatch', *Guardian*, Online section, 19 December 1996.

105. Bowen, D., 'Why the world answers your local phone call', *Independent on Sunday*, 13 April 1997.

106. Stanislaw, L., *The Cyberiad: Fables of the Cybernetic Age*, Harvest Books, 1985.

107. *Communications Overload*, Gallup, the Institute of the Future and San Jose University, USA, spring 1997.

108. As quoted in Bailey, E., 'Communications stress: it's time to pull the plug', *Independent on Sunday*, 13 July 1997.

109. Toffler, A., *The Third Wave*, William Morrow, New York, USA, 1980.

110. Tapscott, D., *The Digital Enterprise: Promise and Peril in the Age of Networked Intelligence*, McGraw-Hill, 1995.

111. Booth, N., 'Fears of a Divided Society', *The Times*, Interface section, 9 July 1997: see also the accompanying articles in the same edition, 'Surviving the future: how to become a successful cybercitizen' and 'Days numbered for tax'.

112. Leadbeater, C., *Britain: the California of Europe? What the UK can learn from the West Coast*, Demos Commentary, May 1997.

113. *California economic growth 1996-97*, Centre for Continuing Study of the Californian Economy, Palo Alto, California, 1997.

114. Rifkin, J., *The End of Work: The Decline of the Global Labor Force and the Dawn of the Post-Market Era*, G P Putnam's Sons Publisher, US, 1995.

115. 'When info worlds collide', *Fortune*, 28 October 1997.

116. Gross, N., 'Into the Wild Frontier', Information Technology Annual Report, *Business Week*, 23 June 1997.

117. 'Jellyfish turns into computer', *Sunday Times*, Innovation section, 27 July 1997.

118. Millar, S., 'Frankenstein's successor: a purple spider with a mind of its own that likes to go walkabout', *Guardian*, 28 July 1997.

119. Gross, N., 'Into the Wild Frontier', Information Technology Annual Report, *Business Week*, 23 June 1997.

120. *Making It In Miniature*, Parlimentary Office of Science and Technology, House of Commons, London, November 1996.

121. Elliott, L., 'Pulling up home roots', *Guardian*, 7 July 1997.

Index